Critical Literacy

A Collection of Articles From the Australian Literacy Educators' Association

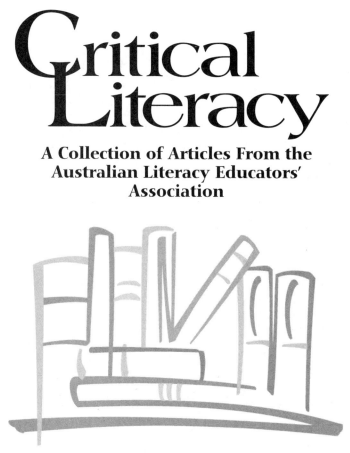

Heather Fehring & Pam Green
Royal Melbourne Institute of Technology University
Bundoora, Victoria, Australia
Editors

INTERNATIONAL
Reading
Association

800 Barksdale Road, PO Box 8139
Newark, Delaware 19714-8139, USA
www.reading.org

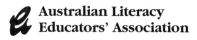
Australian Literacy
Educators' Association

PO Box 3203
Norwood
South Australia 5067, Australia

The International Reading Association attempts, through its publications, to provide a forum for a wide spectrum of opinions on reading. This policy permits divergent viewpoints without implying the endorsement of the Association.

Director of Publications Joan M. Irwin
Editorial Director, Books and Special Projects Matthew W. Baker
Special Projects Editor Tori Mello Bachman
Permissions Editor Janet S. Parrack
Associate Editor Jeanine K. McGann
Production Editor Shannon Benner
Publications Coordinator Beth Doughty
Production Department Manager Iona Sauscermen
Art Director Boni Nash
Supervisor, Electronic Publishing Anette Schütz-Ruff
Electronic Publishing Specialist Cheryl J. Strum

Project Editor Matthew W. Baker

Library of Congress Cataloging in Publication Data
    Critical literacy: a collection of articles from the Australian Literacy Educators' Association/Heather Fehring, Pam Green, editors.
        p.   cm.
Articles were originally published between 1990 and 2000.
Includes bibliographical references.
    ISBN 0-87207-286-X
1. Language arts–Social aspects–Australia.   2. Literacy–Social aspects–Australia.
3. Critical pedagogy–Australia.   I. Fehring, Heather.   II. Green, Pam.   III. Australian Literacy Educators' Association.
LB1576.C78   2001
370.11'5–dc21   00-012469

Printed in Canada

Contents

Contributors

Editors

Heather Fehring
Senior Lecturer
Department of School and Early
    Childhood Education
Faculty of Education, Language
    and Community Services
RMIT University
Bundoora, Victoria, Australia

Pam Green
Senior Lecturer
Faculty of Education, Language
    and Community Services
RMIT University
Bundoora, Victoria, Australia

Authors

Carolyn D. Baker
Associate Professor
Graduate School of Education
The University of Queensland
St. Lucia, Brisbane, Queensland,
    Australia

Barbara Comber
Director, Centre for Studies in
    Literacy, Policy and Learning
    Cultures
School of Education
University of South Australia
Underdale, South Australia,
    Australia

Cal Durrant
Lecturer in English Curriculum
    and Media Education
Australian Institute of Education
Murdoch University
Murdoch, Western Australia,
    Australia

Peter Freebody
Professor
Department of Cognition,
    Language and Special Education
Griffith University, Mt Gravatt
    Campus
Brisbane, Queensland, Australia

James Paul Gee
Professor
Department of Instruction and
    Communication
University of Wisconsin
Madison, Wisconsin, USA

Pam Gilbert
Professor of Education
School of Education
James Cook University
Townsville, Queensland, Australia

Bill Green
Professor of Education
School of Curriculum Studies
Faculty of Education, Health and
    Professional Studies
University of New England
Armidale, New South Wales,
    Australia

Anne Hanzl
Children's literature consultant
Mont Albert North, Victoria,
    Australia

Ann Kempe
Toowoomba Education Centre
Toowoomba, Queensland,
    Australia

Allan Luke
Professor and Head of School
Graduate School of Education
Faculty of Social and Behavioural
    Sciences
The University of Queensland
Brisbane, Queensland, Australia

Jennifer O'Brien
Medindie Gardens,
South Australia, Australia

Michael Singh
Professor and Head of Department
Language and International Studies
Faculty of Education, Language
    and Community Services
RMIT University
Melbourne, Victoria, Australia

Karen van Harskamp-Smith
Secondary school teacher
Bwgcolman Community School
Palm Island, Queensland, Australia

Stephen van Harskamp-Smith
Secondary school teacher
Bwgcolman Community School
Palm Island, Queensland, Australia

Grant Webb
Principal Education Officer,
    Mackay Hinterland
Education Department of
    Queensland
Mackay, Queensland, Australia

Lorraine Wilson
Education consultant
North Carlton, Victoria, Australia

Introduction

The emergence of critical literacy in the late 1980s and early 1990s expanded, yet again, teachers' knowledge of influences that enhance literacy development. As a reader and a writer it is important to understand the many influences that impinge on the reading and writing processes. We must not only understand how the language is constructed, but also how language is used to influence readers in different ways. Readers interpret texts from their own sociocultural values and thus the same text may have multiple meanings depending on readers' perspectives.

Critical literacy theorists and practitioners have added a new dimension to our understanding of the theoretical underpinnings of literacy acquisition and to the classroom practices we use to implement these new understandings. The authors represented in this collection of articles challenge us to reflect on the literacy practices and texts that we choose to use in our classrooms.

The collection includes one new piece that begins the book and 11 previously published articles. The previously published articles were selected using the following criteria:

- The articles were published by the Australian Literacy Educators' Association (ALEA) between 1990 and 2000.
- Some articles explain the principles of critical literacy from a theoretical perspective.
- Some articles illustrate the comparative changes between theories of literacy development.
- Some articles detail the practical classroom implementation of critical literacy principles.
- All articles highlight the changing role of the teacher in the process of students coming to understand the multiple meanings of texts and the power of language.

The 12 articles are as follows:

Green, P. "Critical literacy revisited"
    Green's article sets the context of critical literacy for this collection of articles. She explores the notion of what critical literacy means and

how this concept became a significant influence on our understanding of the changing nature of literacy in the 1980s and 1990s. Literacy is an empowering attribute if readers and writers become aware of how texts are constructed and how such constructions influence their perspectives of the world. Green encourages teachers to instigate classroom practices that facilitate students to actively engage in critically analyzing a range of text types. Such practices will empower students to understand the world in which they live.

Gee, J.P. (1993). "Critical literacy/socially perceptive literacy: A study of language in action"

Gee's article, though conceptually complex, is a thought-provoking narrative exploring the meaning of the term *critical literacy*, which he calls *socially perceptive literacy*. Taking a linguistic stance Gee deconstructs a piece of conversation from a speaker and a listener's perspective. Using this example Gee illustrates and examines three key properties of human language—"social gravity," "speakers dilemma," and "multiple coding"—as language is used in context.

Kempe, A. (1993). "No single meaning: Empowering students to construct socially critical readings of the text"

Kempe's article highlights the notion that readers need to be agents of social change. To be able to undertake such responsibility readers need to be critically literate and become conscious of the notion of texts containing multiple meanings. She outlines a framework of a Year 7 (post-primary schooling) unit of work related to textual representation of gender. The article includes exemplary texts that provide a wide range of thought-provoking interpretations, teaching strategies, and examples of questioning techniques that encourage self-awareness of one's own reading practices.

Kempe encourages teachers to deconstruct their own teaching practices in order to maximise the empowering ability of informed choice for their students.

Baker, C.D., & Freebody, P. (1993). "The crediting of literate competence in classroom talk"

Baker and Freebody illustrate how the literacy classroom is a political environment. Using examples from teacher–student talk and questioning, they demonstrate how students learn what values and beliefs "count" in the world of literacy. Their article highlights the need for teachers to be continually aware that the curriculum we design is never neutral. As teachers we must be conscious of, and constantly challenging, the values, beliefs, and judgements we present to our students in the course of literacy instruction.

Gilbert, P. (1993). "(Sub)versions: Using sexist language practices to explore critical literacy"
> Gilbert's article challenges readers to recognise the inequitable literacy practices in our own teaching. The social construction of gender in the texts and the language practices we use in schools can be exposed effectively by taking a critical literacy stance. Gilbert proposes that as teachers we develop a variety of strategies to examine texts from multiple perspectives and encourage discussion of the social and cultural values readers bring to texts.

Hanzl. A. (1993). "Critical literacy and children's literature: Exploring the story of Aladdin"
> Hanzl's article demonstrates that even the simplest of children's stories carry messages about the bias and culture of the author and the illustrator. However, she encourages teachers to explore children's interpretations and by doing so awaken children to the issues at the heart of critical literacy: issues of gender, race, and cultural stereotyping; issues of power and disempowerment; and issues encompassed in the social creation of "reality."

Comber, B. (1993). "Classroom explorations in critical literacy"
> Comber's article looks at critical literacy within two primary classrooms in terms of the problematising of classroom texts. The classroom scenarios described are lively and demonstrate key elements of critical approaches theory in practice. A series of critical questions are raised in order to explore the nature of classroom practice in which critical literacy approaches are adopted. Three principles guiding approaches to critical literacy are reiterated as the author reminds us of the need to rethink and redefine critical literacy in practice.

van Harskamp-Smith, S., & van Harskamp-Smith, K. (1994). "Torres Strait Islanders speak: Building a model of critical literacy"
> The authors present the educational concerns of key stakeholders involved in the education of Torres Strait Islanders. It is argued that

critical literacy provides a valuable orientation for people in Maganiu Mala Kes (the Torres Strait Islands) who are looking toward an education that encompasses traditional language and culture but also involves the acquisition of English literacy and numeracy. The need for teachers to work with students to build a metalanguage of criticism is highlighted as is the need for teachers to take into account the cultural/political nature of literacy and the ramifications of uncritical imposed curriculum. A critical literacy framework revised in keeping with the islanders' ways is seen as a means to move toward empowerment in the development of relevant curriculum.

Luke, A., O'Brien, J., & Comber, B. (1994). "Making community texts objects of study"
The article explores the challenge involved in working with everyday community texts in ways that engage students in the study of how texts work. The authors provide a framework for critical literacy practices in which students move beyond a technical analysis of language to also read the cultures surrounding the text. The presentation of three instances of classroom practice in which community texts are analysed critically shows the benefits of such work. An argument for teaching that goes beyond mere language awareness and incorporates critical literacy practices that help students move beyond a "taken-for-granted" view of the world is made strongly and convincingly.

Webb, G., & Singh, M. (1998). "'…and what about the boys?' Re-reading signs of masculinities"
Webb and Singh focus on notions of masculinity and education with a view to challenge what tends to be largely taken for granted: the ways in which gender is constructed within texts. The authors use critical literacy practices to problematise school texts and notions of masculinity. A call is made for the explicit teaching of students in re-reading and rewriting school texts from various viewpoints, in particular from the perspective of "the self-critical pro-feminist man." Such action is seen as a starting point for critiques of men's practices and oppressive models of masculinities, which contribute to the struggle against sexism, patriarchy, and literacy problems.

Wilson, L. (1999). "Critical literacy and pop music magazines"
Wilson's practically based article highlights critical literacy in action through an integrated unit of work on pop music magazines.

Although the role of text analyst was the focus of the unit, the students took on the other roles within Freebody and Luke's framework for readers' roles and worked as code breakers, text participants, and text users. Although such roles are not explicated here, the article provides a glimpse of students who were challenged to view writers as being anything but neutral.

Durrant, C., & Green, B. (2000). "Literacy and the new technologies in school education: Meeting the l(IT)eracy challenge?"

Bridging the knowledge of informational technology (IT) and critical literacy best summarizes this article. Acknowledging that to be "literate" is in a constant state of flux, Durrant and Green explore the ramifications of the educational convergence of literacies and technologies. The article examines a model for curriculum integration whereby the sociocultural perspectives on literacy, informational technology, and schooling complement each other to produce a rich interactive framework of school literacy practices. The model incorporates three dimensions of literacy-technology learning and practice: the operational (functional and technological knowledge), the cultural (contextual knowledge), and the critical (critical analytical knowledge).

The Appendix is a collection of book reviews related to critical literacy. The books reviewed are as follows:

Stephens, J. (1992). *Language and ideology in children's fiction*

Janks, H. (1993). *Language & position and language, identity and power*

Burns, A., & Hood, S. (1998). *Teaching critical literacy* (Teachers' Voices 3)

Knobel, M., & Healy, A. (Eds). (1998). *Critical literacies in the primary classroom*

Lohrey, A. (1998). *Critical literacy: A professional development resource*

Dally, S. (1998). *Civics and citizenship: we will take part: Teaching civics and citizenship* and the companion glossary *The ABC of being a critically literate citizen*

Barton, D., Hamilton, M., & Ivanic, R. (Eds.). (1999). *Situated literacies: Reading and writing in context*

Critical literacy has the potential to give students the opportunity to read the world so that they can read the word. This collection of articles is testimony to such potential, and provides a range of instances in which theory meets practice from a multiplicity of perspectives on critical literacy.

Heather Fehring
Pam Green

Critical Literacy Revisited
Pam Green

The need for a critical stance with respect to literacy has long been argued by researchers, such as Freire (1970, 1973, 1983, 1985), Gilbert (1989a,b,c; 1990; 1993a,b,c), Krevotics (1985), Lankshear (1993), and Withers (1989). For instance, Withers states,

> We are long beyond the stage of accepting basic literacy—the ability to read and write one's own name—as the norm for the general population. We have also passed beyond the stage of wanting functional literacy for all—a set of relatively simple abilities to comprehend and produce written text at home, in the streets and in the workplace. What we have come to realise is needed is "critical literacy"...the direction of those functional skills towards the ability to mount a personal critique of all those issues which surround us as we live, learn and work—to help us understand, comment on and ultimately control the direction of our lives. (p. 76)

Notions central to critical literacy approaches

In recent years, particularly in the late 1980s and early 1990s, notions of critical literacy have emerged. However, what constitutes critical literacy varies within the literature. According to Knoblauch and Brannon (1993), the "sources of critical literacy and pedagogy are to be found in an assortment of Marxist, feminist, and postmodern intellectual positions" (p. 161). Lankshear (1994) does not see the sources as quite as clear-cut. In fact, he states that the calls for critical literacy come from "quite disparate theoretical positions; or, from no discernible theoretical position at all" (p. 4).

According to Donald (1993), the stance taken in terms of critical literacy depends on the kinds of questions that are asked. Comber (1993) takes a similar view and notes different orientations within the many forms that critical literacy can take. Each orientation has its own principles guiding the approach to critical literacy. These principles include repositioning students as researchers of language, respecting minority culture literacy practices, and problematising classroom and public texts. Arguably such principles do not account for all possibilities within critical literacy.

Furthermore, there may be overlap among the three. For instance, it is possible to place students in the position of language researchers by looking at available classroom texts with respect to how a particular minority group is represented. What becomes clear from the literature, therefore, is that critical literacy is a "contested educational ideal" and that there is "no final orthodoxy of critical literacy" (Lankshear, 1994, p. 4).

Despite the complexities about what such a critical literacy stance might entail, there are some common notions found in the general literature. The notions of text, literacy as social practice, and discourse, which have been discussed within cultural literacy, are also integral to critical literacy. For instance, Lankshear (1994) points out that critical literacy may involve a number of objects of critique, such as knowing literacy (or various literacies) critically, viewing particular texts critically, and/or having a critical perspective on the social practices involved in literacy use. Thus, text and literacy as social practices are highlighted within critical literacy.

A double-edged sword

The two-sided nature of literacy is a notion inherent to critical literacy. Literacy can be seen as a double-edged sword in that it can be enlightening or liberating but also may be restrictive or dominating (Edelsky & Harman, 1991; Shannon, 1992). In other words, there is a duality about literacy. For instance, within the context of the school, literacy can limit students. When textbooks are selected that portray a mainstream view of the world, and when traditional literacy practices, which often reduce literacy to copying and the completion of worksheets or assignment questions, are used, literacy is far from liberating. Instead, such curricula "tend to maintain, rather than improve, the status of subordinant [sic] groups" (Harman & Edelsky, 1989, p. 393). Furthermore, being able to "construct and make meaning from text may appear empowering, but in fact may open one to multiple channels of misinformation and exploitation: You may just become literate enough to get yourself badly in debt, exploited and locked out" (Luke, 1992, p. 19). Thus, literacy is not necessarily liberating, and it may be exploitative. This notion is central to critical literacy.

Literacy and empowerment

The metaphor of a double-edged sword is useful in that it serves to temper grandiose claims in which literacy is associated with "empowerment." As noted earlier, although there may be potential for liberation or empowerment, whether or not this is realised depends on many factors. For example, "Freire believes that literacy empowers people only when it renders them active questioners of the social reality around them" (Gee, 1989, p. 161). However, whether or not being an active questioner is sufficient to gain power is questionable. Although taking a critical stance may unravel or expose the power base of the society, it does not necessarily provide access to it. Robinson (1988) points out, "to achieve literacy does not necessarily earn one power, as we well know. But the powerful are usually themselves literate, or if not, they can purchase the services of those who are" (pp. 244–245). Thus, although being literate, and in particular adopting a critical stance with respect to literacy, may be seen as liberating or empowering, it does not afford any guarantees. As Luke (1992–1993) states,

> Literacy is a necessary but not sufficient condition for participation and enfranchisement. While the human capital model doesn't work, literacy remains a significant gatekeeping factor in the everyday lives of Australians. In the current situation, not having credentialled levels of literate competence will increasingly lead to marginalisation. But having high levels of credentialled literacy doesn't necessarily lead to employment, power or wealth—for individuals or the nation. Literacy thus has become a kind of double-bind: Having it doesn't guarantee anything, but not having it systematically excludes one from cultural and economic power. (p. 21)

At this point, the need to consider what is meant by empowerment is apparent. What is considered empowerment is problematic (Gore, 1991; Lather, 1992), because the term is used in various ways within the literature. For instance, Simon (1992) states, "Empowerment literally means to give ability to, to permit or enable" (p. 143). He notes that this entails enabling students to use their own cultural resources and to explain the relationship between school and society. According to Fletcher (1987), empowerment refers to "a process which alters the individual's perception of themselves [sic] and the society in a particular way" (p. 10). Although these uses of the term *empowerment* acknowledge to varying degrees the individual and social aspects of power, they fail to explain them fully. As I have stated elsewhere,

> The term *empowerment* is overused and often misused. It is misleading in that it creates images of social power, and whilst being able to read and to write enables the individual to function within our society, we do not gain access to the power bases of society just because we can read and write. (Green, 1992, p. 16)

The work of Delpit (1991) is useful here in that she distinguishes individual and social aspects of power in relation to literacy. She makes the distinction between personal literacy (literacy for one's own entertainment, thinking, emotions, and life) and power code literacy (literacy that gives access to the world beyond the personal). Delpit explains how some students have access to power as their intimates (those with whom they interact) are part of the culture of power, but for some access is blocked as their intimates are not part of that culture. Thus, it is apparent that although personal literacy may enable certain uses of language, it does not necessarily empower in terms of the power bases within society. Furthermore, even if access is achieved it is not free from the impact of the ideologies that control the kinds of literacies that are deemed powerful.

What a critical literacy perspective entails

Now that clarification of notions that are central to critical literacy has been offered, I will consider what a critical stance to literacy might entail. A critical perspective of literacy argues for an active, challenging approach to literacy. Exponents of critical literacy assert various potentials of such a perspective. One such potential pertains to the critical reading of texts, which can enable students to become aware of the way in which texts are constructed and how such constructions position the reader (Bigelow, 1992; Freebody & Luke, 1990; Luke 1992, 1995). This potential leads us to the role of writing in critical literacy and therefore the connections between reading and writing.

The links between reading and writing are clearly evident in the literature. According to a number of researchers, including Freire (1983, 1985), Gilbert (1989a,b,c; 1990; 1993a,b,c), Green (1988), Kress (1985), and Rivalland (1989), the most effective way to develop critical readers is through writing. Such approaches to literacy offer potential for students to understand how language works, the ways in which various individuals and groups use literacy to their own ends, and the reasons behind such use. Furthermore, educators have the potential to critically examine what counts as literacy, the way in which texts are used, and the literacy demands made on students. In this way a critical approach to literacy has potential for the student and for educators. However, whether or not such potential is realised depends on the complexities involved in the context in which literacy occurs.

Critical literacy also offers potential for literacy across subject areas. There is a growing body of literature in this area (see, for example, Comber, Barnett, Badger, & Peters, 1991; Elkins, 1989; Freebody, 1989); at this point Green's (1988) work is used to summarize the potential of a critical perspective in this respect:

> A socially critical stance on subject-specific literacy means providing individuals, at any level of schooling, with the means to reflect critically on what is being learned and taught in classrooms and to take an active role in the production of knowledge and meaning. It involves giving individuals the capacity to recognise the socially constructed and conventional nature of school knowledge, and to work collaboratively and constructively towards informed personal meanings. (p. 163)

The example of reading a textbook illustrates what such a stance entails. Green points out,

> Rather than the single, authorised version of the textbook, for instance, students should have the capacity and be given the opportunity to consult different and sometimes conflicting sources of information, in order to arrive at personal understandings. The literate individual is someone who knows that there is more than one version available, and that what one is reading, or is given to read, represents both a selection and an abstraction from a larger context. (p. 63)

Thus, the juxtapositioning of texts (reading a range of texts on a given subject or topic) arguably enables students to perceive a range of viewpoints and to consider each in a critical way. Green continues to say that when students have the opportunity to make links between what is new and what is familiar, learning becomes more meaningful and school knowledge is transformed into active knowledge.

Critical literacy in the classroom

Although clearly a number of potentials exist within critical literacy, the translation of such theory into practice is not easy. For instance, Gilbert (1993a) alerts us to the difficulties associated with implementing critical literacy in the classroom. She admits that

> classroom practices that will engage students with the social context of literacy are difficult to construct and to enact. The social context of literacy learning has still, as work by Kress (1985), or Gee (1990), or Luke (1993) amply demonstrates, some distance to travel in classrooms, because the issues associated with a "criti-

cal" literacy are complex. How, for instance, can students learn about the social context of language, unless they are able to experience the impact of actual language practices in contexts that are of interest and concern to them? (p. 324)

Within the context of the classroom, critical literacy offers a critical approach to text, a language of critique or a critical discourse, and examination of literacy across content areas. However, before critical literacy can occur within the classroom, students need the opportunity to engage in meaningful use of literacy, or in other words, to use literacy in ways that relate to their interests and needs. Without the opportunity to write and read for a range of purposes, with access to a variety of texts, there is no basis upon which critical discussion of and reflection on literacy can occur. Such opportunities are essential if students are to begin to examine the ways in which texts are constructed, and for what purposes.

REFERENCES

Bigelow, W. (1992). Once upon a genocide: Christopher Columbus in children's literature. *Language Arts, 69*, 112–120.

Comber, B. (1993). Literacy and social justice. In A. Reid & B. Johnson (Eds.), *Critical issues in Australian education in the 1990s* (pp. 112–124). Adelaide, Australia: Painter Prints.

Comber, B., Barnett, J., Badger, L., & Peters, J. (1991). *Literacy and language professional development in disadvantaged schools: A statewide survey.* Adelaide, Australia: University of South Australia.

Delpit, L. (1991). A conversation with Lisa Delpit. *Language Arts, 68*, 541–547.

Donald, J. (1993). Literacy and the limits of democracy. In B. Green (Ed.), *The insistence of the letter: Literacy studies and curriculum theorizing* (pp. 120–136). London: Falmer Press.

Edelsky, C., & Harman, S. (1991). Risks and possibilities of whole language literacy: Alienation and connection. In C. Edelsky (Ed.), *With literacy and justice for all: Rethinking the social in language and education* (pp. 127–140). London: Falmer Press.

Elkins, J. (1989). Literacy and transition to secondary school. *Australian Journal of Reading, 12*(4), 300–305.

Fletcher, R. (1987). Empowerment and adult education. *Australian Journal of Adult Education, 27*(1), 9–12.

Freebody, P. (1987). What counts as "knowing content"? *Australian Journal of Reading, 12*(4), 330–338.

Freebody, P., & Luke, A. (1990). "Literacies" programs: Debates and demands in cultural context. *Prospect, 5*(3), 7–16.

Freire, P. (1970). *Pedagogy of the oppressed.* New York: Herder and Herder.

Freire, P. (1973). *Education for critical consciousness.* New York: The Seabury Press.

Freire, P. (1983). The importance of the act of reading. *Journal of Education, 165*(1), 5–11.

Freire, P. (1985). Reading the world and reading the word: An interview with Paulo Freire. *Language Arts, 62*(1), 15–21.

Gee, J.P. (1989). The legacies of literacy: From Plato to Freire through Harvey Graff. *Journal of Education, 171*(1), 147–165.

Gee, J.P. (1990). *Social linguistics and literacies: Ideology in discourses.* London: Falmer Press.

Gilbert, P. (1989a). *Writing, schooling, and deconstruction: From voice to text in the classroom.* London: Routledge.

Gilbert, P. (1989b). Stoning the romance: Girls as resistant readers and writers. In *Writing in schools: Reader* (pp. 73–80). Geelong, Australia: Deakin University Press.

Gilbert, P. (1989c). Student text as pedagogical text. In S. de Castell, A. Luke, & C. Luke (Eds.), *Language, authority and criticism: Readings on the school textbook* (pp. 195–202). London: Falmer Press.

Gilbert, P. (1990). Personal growth or critical resistance? Self-esteem in the English curriculum. In J. Kenway & S. Willis (Eds.), *Hearts and minds: Self-esteem and the schooling of girls* (pp. 173–189). London: Falmer Press.

Gilbert, P. (1993a). (Sub)versions: Using sexist language practices to explore critical literacy. *The Australian Journal of Language and Literacy, 16*(4), 323–331.

Gilbert, P. (1993b). Introduction. In P. Gilbert (Ed.), *Gender stories and the language classroom* (pp. 1–36). Geelong, Australia: Deakin University Press.

Gilbert, P. (1993c). Dolly fiction(s): Teen romances downunder. In P. Gilbert (Ed.), *Gender stories and the language classroom* (pp. 66–85). Geelong, Australia: Deakin University Press.

Gore, J. (1991). Neglected practices: A foucaldian critique of traditional and radical approaches to pedagogy. In *The Liberating Curriculum Conference, Paper 21* (pp. 2–13). Adelaide, Australia: Australian Curriculum Studies Association.

Green, B. (1988). Subject-specific literacy and school learning: A focus on writing. *Australian Journal of Education, 32*(2), 156–179.

Green, P. (1992). *A matter of fact: Using factual texts in the classroom.* Melbourne, Australia: Eleanor Curtain.

Harman, S., & Edelsky, C. (1989). The risks of whole language literacy: Alienation and connection. *Language Arts, 66*(4), 392–406.

Knoblauch, C.H., & Brannon, L. (1993). *Critical teaching and the idea of literacy.* Portsmouth, NH: Boyton/Cook.

Kress, G. (1985). *Linguistic processes in sociocultural practice.* Geelong, Australia: Deakin University Press.

Krevotics, J. (1985). Critical literacy: Challenging the assumptions of mainstream educational theory. *Journal of Education, 167*(2), 50–62.

Lankshear, C. (1993). Curriculum as literacy: Reading and writing in "New Times." In B. Green (Ed.), *The insistence of the letter: Literacy studies and curriculum theorizing* (pp. 154–174). London: Falmer Press.

Lankshear, C. (1994). *Critical literacy.* Canberra, Australia: Australian Curriculum Studies Association.

Lather, P. (1992). Post-critical pedagogies: A feminist reading. In C. Luke & J. Gore (Eds.), *Feminisms and critical pedagogy* (pp. 120–137). London: Routledge.

Luke, A. (1992). *When basic skills and information processing just aren't enough: Rethinking reading in new times* (A.J.A. Nelson Address of the 1992 National Conference of the

Australian Council for Adult Literacy, pp. 1–24). Townsville, North Queensland, Australia: Australian Council for Adult Literacy.

Luke, A. (1992–1993). Literacy and human capital: Rethinking the equation. *Education Australia, 19-20*, 19–21.

Luke, A. (1993). Stories of social regulation: The micropolitics of classroom narrative. In B. Green (Ed.), *The insistence of the letter: Literacy studies and curriculum theorizing* (pp. 137–153). London: Falmer Press.

Luke, A. (1995). The social practice of reading. In J. Murray (Ed.), *Celebrating differences: Confronting literacies* (pp. 167–187). Sydney, Australia: Australian Reading Association.

Rivalland, J. (1989). Meaningmaking: A juggling act. *Australian Journal of Literacy, 12*(4), 5–21.

Robinson, J.L. (1988). The social context of literacy. In E.R. Kintgen, B.M. Kroll, & M. Rose (Eds.), *Perspectives on literacy* (pp. 243–253). Carbondale, IL: Southern Illinois University Press.

Shannon, P. (1992). Why become political? In P. Shannon (Ed.), *Becoming political: Readings and writings in the politics of literacy education* (pp. 1-11). Portsmouth, NH: Heinemann.

Simon, R.I. (1992). Empowerment as a pedagogy of possibility. In P. Shannon (Ed.), *Becoming political: Readings and writings in the politics of literacy education* (pp. 139–151). Portsmouth, NH: Heinemann.

Withers, G. (1989). Three versions of "critical literacy." *English in Australia, 89*, 72–79.

Critical Literacy/Socially Perceptive Literacy: A Study of Language in Action

James Paul Gee

T wo of the most common meanings of the phrase "critical literacy" are: a literacy for "higher-order thinking"—thinking that counts as "intelligent" to experts (Graubard, 1991; Resnick, 1987); and a literacy for social and political criticism ("critique"), including criticism of what counts as "higher-order thinking" to experts and other elites (Giroux, 1992; Stuckey, 1991). I will not here be concerned with "critical literacy" in either of these—admittedly important—senses. Rather, I will argue that language creates, for us humans, a problem, one that becomes acute in pluralistic societies and in institutional settings. After delineating this problem, I will define the sort of "critical literacy" I am interested in as a literacy for dealing with it. Since the term "critical literacy" has so many meanings, I will replace it, as far as my interests are concerned, with the term "socially perceptive literacy."

I will develop my argument by closely attending to one example. I do this because, as a linguist, I find concrete examples good tools with which to theorize. But I mean my example to stand for more generally applicable points. You will need a bit of background to understand the example. It comes from the first formal meeting of a project sponsored by an educational research institute and carried out in a medium size post-industrial town on the east coast of the United States. The institute, however, was housed in a large, metropolitan (and much more prestigious) city forty miles away. The meeting was attended by a researcher from the institute, several undergraduate and graduate students assisting her, six elementary

From the *Australian Journal of Language and Literacy*, 16(4), November 1993. Reprinted with permission of the author and the Australian Literacy Educators' Association.

school history and social science teachers, two curriculum consultants, and one young, but well-known, university (associate) professor of history.

The historian and the students were connected to a local, prestigious private university. They, the researcher, and the curriculum consultants were middle or upper-middle-class people, none of whom were born in the town where the project was carried out. Those who did live there—given the upward mobility of such professionals—are likely not to live there in the future. The teachers were women from working-class families, born and raised in or around the town. They had used teaching as a way to enter the local middle class, with some attendant disappointment given the progressive (though, by no means, complete) deterioration of the town and of their social status attendant on contemporary demographic and economic changes.

There were two goals to the project: first, to improve history teaching and curriculum in the schools by bringing teachers, educational researchers, curriculum experts, and "real" historians together; second, to allow the research institute not only to assist with this effort, but to do research on language and interaction within teacher-researcher-university collaborations. Both of these are currently popular agendas within the national United States debate on the quality of education (Brown, 1991).

Let me hasten to add, that, of course, this is a "post-hoc" summary. The project lasted for several months, and was never quite this simple. Furthermore, the project—as so many others like it—eventually issued in rather transitory results, no significant long-term improvements, and in mutual attributions (albeit rather mild) of hidden agendas, ill will, misunderstandings and/or lack of intelligence to which problems were easily attributable. All in all, it was a rather typical institutional encounter—people came together, accomplished less than might be hoped, disbanded, and counted the endeavour more or less a "success" marred by the all too human foibles of self-interest, misunderstanding, and less than exemplary competence (Dow, 1991; Moffett, 1988).

We will concentrate on only one sentence—part of the opening remarks by the representative of the research institute. We will refer to this young woman by the pseudonym "Ariel Dante." After suggesting that everyone at the meeting introduce themselves, Ariel says, "I'm Ariel Dante from the Literacy Centre" (also a pseudonym), and then utters the sentence below:

> I'm sort of taking up a part of co-ordinating this project, bringing the two schools together, and trying to um look at how ah how we organize, well what we're go-

ing to do in these meetings, what it means for teachers and researchers and historians and curriculum people to come on and try to organize a team and students interested in history and other things, to try to organize a team to get a
piece of curriculum essentially up and running and working in the schools.

Out of this context this looks innocent enough a rather mundane
piece of institutional language. My point will be that in context especially
institutional contexts language is never innocent.

Social gravity

I want to argue that there is a "problem" with everyday, normal communication, one that becomes acute in institutional settings. This problem
stems from several key properties of human language as it is used in context. First I will develop these properties—"social gravity," "the speaker's
dilemma," and "multiple coding"—then show how they work together to
give rise to difficulties for Ariel, and, finally, state the problem these difficulties reflect. In the end, I will turn to socially perceptive literacy. Let us
start, then, with the property of "social gravity."

I will use the term *actants* for the "things" we talk about, things that are
"out there" in "reality" or sufficiently tied down by previous discourse to be
treated as if they were (Latour, 1987). Not uncommonly people agree there
are actants to be talked about, but do not agree on how to talk about them,
e.g., one party may call a given actant "a freedom fighter" and another
may call the "same" actant "a terrorist." In Figure 1 I list the noun phrases in
Ariel's sentence that indicate actants. We can always consider the speaker
(or writer and/or narrator)—"I"—and the listeners (or readers and/or "implied readers")—"you"—to be actants as well.

There are more or less typical or expectable ways in which these sorts
of actants (or, at least, some of them) are *thought* by people in particular social or cultural groups to be related in the world. There are also more or
less typical or expectable ways in which these actants are verbally identified and related to each other when they are talked about by people from
particular social or cultural groups.

When a set of relationships among a group of actants is considered
typical or expectable to a particular social or cultural group, I will say
that this set of relationships constitutes for a group a *cultural* model—for
example, different social and culture groups have different cultural models for what constitutes typical or expected relationships between hus-
bands and wives, or parents and children (D'Andrande & Strauss, 1992;

FIGURE 1
Noun phrases indicating
actants in Ariel's sentence

I (Ariel) (implies also a "you"), we
a part of this project, this project
the two schools
these meetings
teachers, researchers, historians, curriculum people
a team
students (interested in history)
history
a piece of curriculum, curriculum
the schools

Holland & Quinn, 1987). When any verbal expression of the identity and relationships among a group of actants is considered typical or expectable to a particular social or cultural group, I will say that this sort of verbal expression is a *verbal model* for that group—for example, in some, perhaps many, social or cultural groups in the United States, verbal expressions like "children obey their parents," "children love their parents," and "parents discipline their children" would be considered expectable in a way in which expressions like "children kill their parents" or "children discipline their parents" would not.

To be a member of a given social or cultural group is to know and/or be able to recognize (consciously or unconsciously) a great many cultural models and verbal models in terms of which that group carries out its activities. To be a member of a pluralistic society is also to be a member of many different social and cultural groups (e.g., African Americans, college professors, baseball fans, etc.), as well as to know and/or recognize a great many cultural and verbal models that one associates (rightly or wrongly) with other groups, and which one may dislike.

The people at the meeting where Ariel uttered her sentence inhabit a shared world based on the history and current state of schools and schooling in their area and in the United States. This history has made "available" certain *cultural models* and *verbal models* of how some of the actants indicated by Ariel's sentence might typically be related and verbalized.

One such available cultural model involves the fact that teachers in the United States have often in the past been disempowered in their relationships with researchers and universities (Apple, 1986; Edelsky, 1991). In terms of this model, knowledge flows from the universities and research centres to teachers and from them to their students in a hierarchical fashion, and each party lower on the hierarchy needs to be led or supervised by the special knowledge of the party next higher.

This cultural model is liable to be associated with verbal models involving expressions where researchers or university professors, *run* or *direct* projects or meetings, where they *help* or *service* teachers, their schools, or their students, or where they *design* curricula, or *improve* teachers and teaching in the *schools*. These sorts of verbal expressions involve researchers and university professors having agency over teachers and schools, and they imply (and sometimes go along with overt expression to the effect) that teachers, students, curricula, and schools are "inadequate" or "bad" or "need to be improved" (by them).

In order to have a name for this cultural model, let's call it "the hierarchy model." Of course, there may be somewhat different versions of the hierarchy model for different groups who use, abuse, or contest it, but it certainly represents at least a family of models with a good deal in common.

There are various senses in which cultural and verbal models can be said to be "available." They are often *available* in the sense that their use, in a certain setting, would be "taken for granted," would seem normal and natural, and go largely unnoticed and unremarked. And, indeed, in the past, and in certain settings still today, a version of the hierarchy model would have been or still is available in much this way in the United States.

In a great many places in the United States today, including the town in which Ariel's sentence was uttered, the hierarchy model of teachers, schools, and universities and its associated verbal models have become "available" in another sense. They are available in the sense of being *salient* through having risen to consciousness and having become a matter of struggle and contestation, thanks to various social, economic, political, and cultural changes.

There are today large numbers of teachers who are suspicious of the power, status, and leadership emanating from the university and research communities (Edelsky, 1991: Ch. 10; Smyth, 1992). There are large numbers of researchers and university professors who say they want more "collaborative" relationships with schools and teachers, and who claim that they are themselves "skeptical" about how much and what sort of knowledge they can claim to have (Ellsworth, 1988; Walkerdine, 1986; Willinsky, 1990). Of course, these changes reflect wider changes in the society as a whole: e.g., the increased desire to "mask" power and status and the growing ambivalence about science, research, and technology (Bauman, 1992; Rose, 1991). And, too, these changes are uneven, contradicted at points by other processes, supported by some people and opposed by others.

Any very direct use of the hierarchy model—in certain parts of the United States—then, is likely to get noticed and remarked upon. Expressions of this cultural model through its associated verbal models by those who accept its values may very well be heavily mitigated (masked), and new or less typical verbalizations of it may have to be found. The verbal expressions of those who oppose its values will be staged in part to overtly contrast with it.

What we have said about cultural and verbal models can illuminate Ariel's situation. She is beginning the first "official" meeting of a project set up by a research institute whose staff (researchers and university professors) claim (sincerely, we can suppose) to contest the hierarchy model, and to espouse less hierarchical and more collaborative visions of teacher-researcher-university relationships. But, nonetheless, for all sorts of reasons we need not belabor now, this institute is implementing a project which, in some significant respects, reflects the hierarchy model.

After all, the institute is funding the project, has recruited the teachers—hierarchically through contacts with their administrators, in fact—has called the meeting, and is paying the researchers, historians and curriculum people (though not the teachers, who have "volunteered" in order to receive "college credit"). However sceptical the institute is about the definitiveness of standard educational research, it nonetheless claims to be interested in "improving" teaching and curricula in the two schools represented at the meeting and in "helping" the teachers—while, at the same time, studying ("doing research on") the schools, the teachers and their students. Furthermore, the primary funder of the institute (a large nationally based foundation) is explicitly concerned with improving teaching and learning in United States schools, in light of national debates on the quality of United States education, debates which are often carried out in terms of the hierarchy model and its associated verbal models.

So Ariel—herself opposed to the hierarchy model—must begin communicating in a setting where that model is "available," in one or other of the above senses—either "taken for granted" or "salient" (depending upon the participants in the meeting, differently for different participants)—and where the "actuality" of the larger context wherein the meeting takes place fits, in significant part, that very model.

This sort of situation is not untypical of communication in institutional settings. Very often, when language is being used in institutional contexts in a pluralistic society, some of the available cultural models are at variance with the values, desires, and goals of at least some of the participants, and, indeed, in some cases, at variance with the institution's stated or official goals, thanks to the complexity of human beings and the inertia of institutions.

The presence of cultural and verbal models, as well as the history and structure of institutions and institutional relationships—of the sort we have just discussed—create what I will call *social gravity*, a structure or geometry to the social space within which communication takes place. Words, deeds, and thoughts are *shaped*, within that space, are pushed and pulled, by the uneven and changing, but powerful socio-historical forces (cultural models and institutions) that have created and that perpetuate that space. And it is these forces, too, that necessitate and define the nature of, and energy required for, resistance, should one not wish to "go with the flow."

The speaker's dilemma

Let us turn now from social gravity to "the speaker's dilemma," a second core property of language in context. Speech is produced in "real" time, "on-line" ("on the fly"), in specific contexts, by creatures whose brains (and speech organs) are built and function in relationship to language and speech in a certain way, e.g., not like a computer (Altmann, 1990; Caplan, 1992; Levelt, 1989). Our everyday "folk" model of speech is that people know what they want to say, have it fully represented somehow in their heads (in some conceptual "language of thought"), and that they "translate" these "ideas" into words, phrases, and sentences. In fact, this is rarely true, and certainly not true in the case of Ariel's sentence.

People indeed, do have some higher-order "idea" of what they want to say before they speak, but often discover the *details* of what they "mean" or "intend to say" *as they say it*. Furthermore, speech is produced (constructed in the brain, and output through the mouth) in small chunks, one at a time, chunks which are often considerably smaller than full sentences, and which rarely reflect the whole "idea" all at once.

The chunks in terms of which speech is produced come by many different names in the research literature, depending upon the theorists who have studied them and their particular interests (Brazil, Coulthard, & Johns, 1980; Chafe, 1980; Gee & Grosjean, 1983; Grosjean & Gee, 1987; Halliday, 1985). I will call them *basic speech units*—"BSUs" for short. Each BSU contains on its last content word a salient change of pitch (and stress) and the words in each BSU are said with an integrated intonational contour.

Figure 2 shows the BSUs in Ariel's sentence. Each one ends on a noticeable "bump" in the overall pitch contour of the sentence (usually a slight rise); the pitch then falls a bit and bumps up again on the last content word of the next BSU (the word containing the bump in each BSU is capitalized in Figure 2). This is true of each BSU in Figure 2 except #6 and the last one, #18. At the end of these, we get a more dramatic change in pitch, not

---

FIGURE 2
Basic speech units (BSUs) in Ariel's sentence

First Intonational Sentence:
1 I'm sort of taking up a PART
2 of coordinating this PROJECT
3 bringing the two schools TOGETHER
4 and trying to um look at HOW
5 ah how we ORGANIZE,
6 well what we're going to do in these MEETINGS //

Second Intonational Sentence:
7 what it means for TEACHERS
8 and RESEARCHERS
9 and HISTORIANS
10 and curriculum PEOPLE
11 to come ON
12 and try to organize a TEAM
13 and students interested in HISTORY
14 and other THINGS
15 to try to organize a TEAM
16 to get a piece of CURRICULUM
17 essentially up and RUNNING
18 and working in the SCHOOLS //

just a bump—in both cases a significant fall in pitch. Such dramatic changes (which can be major falls or rises in pitch or combinations of these) announce a *closure*, the fact that the speaker has finished (or, at least momentarily thinks she has finished) a coherent part of the communication (for instance, made a claim or announcement, asked a question or expressed an emotion). All the BSUs up to such a major pitch change constitute an *intonational sentence*. Thus, Ariel's sentence is made up of two intonational sentences: the BSUs 1 through 6, and the BSUs 7 through 18. I place a double slash ("//") at the end of each BSU that ends an intonational sentence by containing a major pitch glide.

Speakers have *some* overall idea (plan) of what they are going to say—for instance, Ariel undoubtedly had "in mind" before and as she spoke an overall "sketch" of what she "intended" to say. Let's call this overall plan, the speaker's *conceptual scheme* (Levelt, 1989). This scheme *may* be very detailed in terms of content (ideas) and *may* even already contain some of the language (verbal expression) that will be used. In the limiting case, one could have memorized what is to be said word for word.

But very often the conceptual scheme will be much less detailed in content and contain no actual language (verbal expressions)—the details and actual language remain to be selected as the speaker outputs one BSU at a time. In these cases, the conceptual scheme is rather like a sketch for a painting that will eventually be much more detailed and filled out in full colour in the actual painting. The actual painting is, of course, produced piece by piece, not all at once—and each piece as it is produced can influence the pieces yet to be produced in ways that go beyond (what could be predicted from) the initial rough sketch.

Speakers linguistically package and output one BSU at a time, actualizing one piece of their conceptual scheme. They probably also have some (not complete and not completely unchangeable as of yet) idea about what the content and linguistic form of their *next* BSU will be. Thus, the content and linguistic encoding of the BSU currently being output can be influenced, to an extent, by the content and linguistic form of the next one. And, of course, all previous BSUs can influence the content and linguistic form of the one being currently produced. The speaker's conceptual scheme influences the content of each BSU, but it is also "filled in" and "extended," even changed, by the specific details of content and linguistic form that gets realized in each successive BSU.

To the extent that the conceptual scheme can be said to represent the speaker's "meaning" and to the extent that it is initially a rough sketch in terms of (somewhat vaguely or abstractly specified) content and contains little or no actual language, the speaker actually discovers more and more specific details about her meaning as she produces each successive BSU.

Thus, in most cases, *what* the speaker has finally said when she has finished an intonational sentence is more detailed and specific in content and language than what she originally intended ("knew"). This is caused by the fact that each BSU may contain specifics of content and language that are more detailed than the conceptual scheme driving their construction, and by the fact that the speaker is influenced, as she is currently constructing a BSU, by the details of what she has said before, and not just by the conceptual scheme.

One of the ways by which the actual output can "out run" the conceptual scheme is as follows (Caplan, 1992; Elman, 1990; Gee, 1992): Say, for example, a speaker utters "I am co-ordinating this project." The word "co-ordinating," having been selected as a realization of some part of the speaker's conceptual scheme, is associated in the speaker's mind with a number of other words and phrases, both in terms of content (e.g., let us say, with "balancing," "organizing," "adjusting," "accommodating," and many more) and in terms of linguistic form (e.g., let us say, with "co-operating," "co-operation," "ordinary," "co-opting," and many more). These associations, now activated, can influence the content and linguistic form of the next BSU (and this one can, in turn, carry over these associations and create new ones that can influence the yet next BSU).

The speaker finds herself, perhaps, uttering "and organizing these meetings" as her next BSU, where the previous "co-ordinating" has helped trigger "organizing," and, perhaps, the previous content and form of "this project" has helped trigger "these meetings" (rather than say "our activities") as the next thing to talk about. These influences go beyond what anyone (including the speaker herself) could have predicted from the initial conceptual scheme prior to knowing how the BSU "I'm co-ordinating this project" was actually going to get said in terms of specific content and linguistic form.

Things would have been different, for example, had the speaker said "I'm directing this research effort"—and conceivably the initial conceptual scheme could have been sketchy enough not to have differentiated between "I'm co-ordinating this project" and "I'm directing this research effort"; something else in the speaker's mind, or the context of communication, may have caused "co-ordinating" to have been selected, rather than "directing."

The upshot of all this is that listeners *can* (though, for various reasons, they many not always do so) attribute to speakers (and speakers themselves can *discover*) detailed and specific "meanings," based on the detailed and specific BSUs and intonational sentences being uttered, meanings which, in a sense, very commonly "out run" speakers' general ideas or plans (conceptual schemes), and which are discovered by speakers in ways not all that dissimilar to the ways in which listeners discover (and interpret) them.

Listeners, of course, form hypotheses about meaning BSU by BSU (they don't wait for the end of the intonational sentence), but they always up-date and fill in these hypotheses as they get more information, based on the detailed and specific linguistic encodings they hear (Gee, 1993). In a sense, listeners (and speakers listening to themselves) are "advantaged" over speakers—they always base their interpretations on detailed linguistic and content codings, rather than the sketchy conceptual schemes that speakers may have begun with. So by the end of an intonational sentence, listeners almost always have at least the potential to have formed a more detailed and specific "meaning" (interpretation) than speakers originally "had in mind" or needed to have "had in mind" at any time other than towards the end of their own utterances.

And, of course, the situation gets "worse"—so to speak—as the speaker utters more and more sentences. The speaker's overall "discourse plan" (the conceptual scheme for several sentences) may be yet more general (less specific and detailed in terms of content of linguistic form) than even individual sentence plans, and its realization affords listeners (including the speaker as listener) more and more specific details of form and content, details that may far "out run" the speaker's original plan or any content the speaker *need* have had "in mind" until much of it has already been output (though, of course, the speaker's plan may get more specifically filled in, more or less ahead of the end of her turn, depending on circumstances, as the speaker "catches on" exactly where she is headed).

This common—but little remarked on and little studied—fact of speaking (Dennett, 1991; Minsky, 1985) has important consequences for speakers, especially in institutional settings. Speakers can easily end up "committed" to details of content and verbal expression that they didn't originally "intend." There is a sense in which speakers come to feel "Oh, so *that's* what I meant" and may also feel, "But do I really want to mean *exactly* that, and what *exactly* does what I've said *imply?*" Speakers can (and do, occasionally) take some of it back, but they can't take *all* of it back, not, at least, if communication is to proceed (and, too, if their credibility is not to be ruined).

Again, this is nothing special—though, of course, the matter can be more or less dramatic in particular instances, depending on how detailed the speaker's original conceptual scheme or discourse scheme was. I will refer to this aspect of the speech situation—that meaning, in a sense, very often "outruns" the speaker's intentions, the speaker's original conceptual scheme—as *the speaker's dilemma*.

The speaker's dilemma is often acute in institutionalized communication. To give one of many reasons why this is so, consider the fact that in such communication, the speaker often has to speak *authoritatively* ("in role") without having had much opportunity to plan (think out) what is to be said or without knowing very clearly what listeners (whose backgrounds one may know little about or share little with) will make of what one has to say (what implications they will draw) once they have heard it in detail (and so have a rich field within which to be pleased or offended).

Multiple coding

Finally, let us turn to the third core property of language in context: *multiple coding*. Every human has multiple identities, identities which are recruited differently in different contexts. For example, Ariel is an advanced graduate student working on her thesis for a prestigious British university; she is an intellectual with a strong interest in the workings of class, culture, and power; she is an educational researcher working for a research institute interested in language in social context and in collaborations between teachers and researchers; she is already a "professional" academic with connections to several universities; she was born and raised on the east coast of the United States and has ties to two ethnic groups (Italian-American and Irish-American); she was raised in the middle class, but went to school with, and was in peer groups with, working class children; she speaks Spanish and has ties to the Hispanic community; and so on through a number of other identities.

Each identity we have represents a characteristic way of being in the world. To enact that identity we think, act, interact, feel, value, and speak (as well as, often, dress) in certain ways, almost as if we are in a play. Such characteristic ways of acting, interacting, thinking, believing, feeling, valuing, dressing, speaking, and so forth, allow us to get *recognised* by—others (and by ourselves) as "*doing* being an X," where X is some identity recognizable by ourselves and others, whether this be "*doing* being an Italian-American (of a certain sort)" or "*doing* being a researcher (of a certain sort)" or "*doing* being a lawyer (of a certain sort)," or whatever (Wieder & Pratt, 1990a, b).

Such socioculturally characteristic ways of being in the world—associations among ways of thinking, feeling, acting, interacting, valuing, speaking, dressing, gesturing, moving, listening, using particular objects (and sometimes writing and reading) that allow people to recognize each other as "*doing* (acting out in thought, word, and deed) being some identity"—I will call *Discourses* with a capital "D" (Gee, 1990). I will use the word "discourse," with a little "d," for language (oral or written) used in context (like Ariel's sentence) and for stretches of language, like stories, arguments, conversations, descriptions, and so forth. Discourses, with a capital "D," recruit discourses, with a little "d," and lots more besides.

There are a great many (and overlapping, sometimes contesting, ever changing, and often mixed) Discourses in any pluralistic society. There are radical feminists, board room executives, workers, African-Americans, Italian-Americans, yuppies, lawyers, linguists, street gangs, fraternity members, literary critics, politicians, soldiers, upper class and lower class people, regulars at a bar, and so on through a nearly endless and never definitive list. People can be members of many, even conflicting, Discourses, can give relatively pure or mixed performances within their Discourses in different contexts, can borrow from one to another, can confuse them, can give them up, actively resist them, parody them, or take overt pride in them.

What people can't do is speak or act meaningfully outside any and all Discourses. Their words or actions would then literally be *unrecognizable*. All words actually uttered or deeds done are rendered meaningful by being placed within one or more Discourses or at the borders of several. The Discourses that make up a society are a grid or framework—a framework that is in people's minds as well as quite overtly out in the world in daily activities and the social structuring of space, time, nature, and objects—against which words and deeds, as well as things (like kittens, babies, and crystals, at least in California), are interpreted, recognized, rendered meaningful.

The "same" objects, people, and locations (settings) can be associated with many different Discourses. This fact gives rise to a property of language in context that I will call *multiple coding*. This property, it turns out, is particularly acute in institutional settings in modern pluralistic societies. Imagine a devout Catholic and an irreligious art historian inside a Catholic church. For the Catholic who has "gone to church," the church is sacred space and each object and person in it is part of her religious Discourse; for the art historian, on a "field trip," let us say, the church and the objects in it are historico-aesthetic objects, caught up in her Discourse in a quite different way. The church and its objects are double coded.

Now imagine the Catholic and the art historian trying to carry on a conversation in the church. Their two Discourses may clash—the Catholic insists on brief whispered snippets of talk, the art historian needs to elaborate her point; or, one may transfer into the other's identity (it turns out the art historian is a lapsed Catholic); or, they may be confused (the Catholic thinks the remark about the statue was said in religious awe, the art historian thinks that the Catholic is ever mindful of her medieval precursors); or a great many other things may happen.

They *may* rise to the "meta-level," so to speak, and discuss how to work out which Discourse the church and its objects will be in for the nonce, but they probably won't. Such meta-level talk can be socially rude (they would have to step outside the church, because the issue of whispering would still arise) and requires yet another common Discourse. Of course, the "problem" of multiple coding can be used strategically as well: the art historian whispers and genuflects during mass and gains access to the church's artistic treasures enacted in a functional context the art historian can analyze.

Multiple coding becomes particularly intricate and complex in institutional settings like the one we are studying here. We have to ask what the *space* meant—the meeting, funded by a research institute and attended by people from the local private university, is being held in an elementary school classroom—and what the *people* meant to each other (as well as what the various objects in the space meant—e.g., the local census-tract documents the historian had brought to the meeting). The space, people, and objects will elicit from each participant various, perhaps multiple, identities from the set of their overall identities (the total ones they are each capable of enacting). The space and people will elicit, as well, confusion, negotiations, and strategies about identities and meanings within their concomitant Discourses.

Ariel's sentence itself, as one multiply coded object among many others in this setting, will "shatter" into a myriad of potential meanings depending upon how it is lined up with the meanings of the people, the space, and objects in the setting, that is, which Discourses they are seen as being in, or, better put, how they are lined up against the framework of multiple Discourses potentially present in the room and even in the society at large.

In institutional settings like the one being discussed here, multiple coding means, in actuality, that there is rarely ever a single, definitive meaning present in anything said, in any action done, in any object present, or in any space of social interaction, and rarely, too, any single and definitive identity for any person present. Meaning is always, so to speak, "up for grabs," changing, negotiable, multiple, potentially usable for strategic purposes—a process and a resource, rather than an established and fixed entity (in or outside "the mind").

The problem in action: Identifying the actants

Having looked at three central properties of language in context, let us turn now to some of the difficulties and complexities these properties created for Ariel and for the project of which she was a part. We start with how she identified her actants.

Ariel must turn the meeting, its participants, and the endeavour they are about to embark on into verbally expressed actants. She faces, in doing this, the speaker's dilemma: she does not know (as she herself claimed later in an interview) exactly what she "wants" to say, what she "should" say, what she "means," however we want to put the matter. She also faces the problem of multiple coding: each of the participants in the meeting has multiple socially relevant identities, and the meetings and the joint endeavour—as well as the space of interaction and the objects present—have potentially many different meanings within different Discourses. Finally, the social gravity created by available cultural and verbal models, as well as the history and structure of institutional relationships (e.g., the uneasy relationships between teachers and researchers on the east coast of the United States), will shape Ariel's words and their meanings even as and if she tries to resist that gravity.

In her first intonational sentence (1–6 in Figure 2), Ariel lexicalizes her actants *deictically*, that is, in terms that directly point to the actual context she is in: this project, the *two* schools, *we, these* meetings. These highly contextualized references trade on the common setting and common knowledge of all the participants, but as such they do very little work towards further identifying the *identities* under which participants in the meeting ("I," "we," "the two schools") are rendered relevant as *actants* (the question: "Why are *you* and *us* actants in this drama?" goes unanswered and begged).

Furthermore, the contextually situated descriptions "this project" and "these meetings," while certainly more contentful than "I" and "we," are still quite general and abstract (What sort of project?, What type of meetings?), quite undetailed outside of the context itself and everyone's assumptions. Of course, this level of generality or something even yet more general may be all that was initially present in Ariel's conceptual scheme.

In her second intonational sentence (7–18 in Figure 2), beginning with "what it means," Ariel attempts to de-contextualize and de-generalize her actants, rendering them more contentful, and, thus, relevant as actants in the drama her sentence is staging. In the second part of her sentence, she recasts "I" and "we" as "teachers and researchers and historians and curriculum people." According to an interview with Ariel after the meeting, she had momentarily forgotten that there were undergraduate and graduate students in the meeting as well, so she later adds "and students interested in history" (and then remembers that not all of the students are primarily focused on history, and so adds "and other things"). These "last minute" additions tell us that Ariel is trying, in fact, to identify the participants in the meeting in terms that will render them relevant actants ("freedom fighters" rather than "those guys").

Ariel's phrases—"teachers and researchers and historians," etc.—involve her immediately in the problem of multiple coding, as almost any attempt to go beyond highly situated references ("I" and "we") would have. Her "add-ons" ("and students interested in history and other things") tell us that all these phrases are meant, in part, to refer specifically to the present participants (who are, after all, teachers, researchers, historians, etc., in terms of some of their socially relevant identities). In this sense, these phrases are tacit definite descriptions (you/we teachers, researchers, historians, etc.).

But Ariel's phrases also are fully interpretable as *generic* descriptions (things like "whales" rather than "those things" or "those whales"), referring to teachers researchers, historians as *types*. Her use of the phrase "the schools" at the end of the sentence trades on the very same ambiguity: it can be taken to mean the specific schools involved in the project or schools as a species of things (as in "We must do something about *the schools*").

In her second intonational sentence Ariel also de-generalizes her earlier "these meetings" and "this project" to spell out *what* these meetings and this project have to do specifically with the specific teachers, researchers, and historians present—or the teachers, researchers, and historians in general as types: they are to become *a team to get a piece of curriculum essentially up and running and working in the schools*. This certainly tells us a lot more about what the "project" is and what the "meetings" will be devoted to. But it also becomes fully caught up with the local tokens or national types: are we primarily dealing with a specific local history curriculum the actual participants in this meeting will come up with or, rather, with the *sort* of curriculum a *representative* group of teachers, historians, and researchers come up with?

Thanks to the double way in which Ariel has lexicalized her actants, each actant—the participants in the meeting, the project, the old and new curriculum, the meetings themselves, the two schools—takes on a *dual significance.* They represent themselves: local teachers, students, curricula, and schools, as well a local university historian (and another local historian involved in the project, but not present at this meeting), for instance, and they serve as "symbols" for the larger issue of teachers, students, curricula, and schools generally.

When Ariel says "what it means for teachers and researchers and historians and curriculum people to come on and...working in the schools," her actants become *both* these people actually present in the context of communication (who are, of course, teachers, researchers, historians, etc., working in two schools) and the general class of teachers, researchers, historians, and so forth, they represent (re-present). The actants (e.g., Ariel as researcher in this project or the specific teacher Karen) here and now become themselves *symbols*, representations of more abstract, general actants (researchers, "the researcher" as type).

The doubleness in Ariel's lexicalization of her actants reflects the fact that the research institute for which Ariel works—and the specific research effort she is formally initiating in this meeting—are both primarily interested not in *these* teachers and schools and their specific curricular problems in the local identities, but in studying them in order to theorize about the general problem of teachers and researchers interacting to "improve" curricula and teaching in the schools.

Even to the extent that the institute and the research effort are directed towards the production of specific practices and a specific curriculum, there must be "exportable" to other places—"models" for use elsewhere—to please the funders of the institute. Most projects like the one Ariel was involved with are carried out in specific places, but are intended to speak to the larger problem of "the schools" or "the education problem" more generally—because that is what funding usually requires and because the researchers and university professors make their careers at a national level by speaking to more global and general issues, rather than mere local circumstances.

Ariel's language captures this problematic—the problematic of working at the local and concrete level while speaking to the global and general level—and, of course, helps to instantiate, reproduce, and actualize it as an issue and a problem. Thus, in a sense, the actants in this project are *these* meetings, *these* teachers, *the* curriculum that exists and the one that will be developed, and the two schools *only* in as much as they *as actants* become "representative"—come to symbolize—another set of actants, namely teachers, students, curricula, and schools in general within the current debate about schools and schooling in the United States. Ariel's sentence, and, in part, the project as a whole, "summon" local identities ("you" as person there in front of me, "you" as Judy or Karen, and "you as teacher in this town") primarily to "recruit" them as symbols at a "higher" level (teachers and the "problem" with "the schools" today).

Furthermore, since this duality of actants triggers the global and general context, as well as the national debate over the "quality of the schools," it also triggers the hierarchical model, a cultural model of schools, teachers, research, and universities which has been prevalent within the national debate on education—a debate which has often been carried out in national and state political life, as well as in the media, in terms of "professionals" improving the quality of teachers, teaching, students, and schools.

It is crucial that the work carried out by this small aspect of Ariel's sentence becomes part of the context for later communication and activity. In this case, we can expect that a particular set of difficulties may arise. It is, in fact, advantageous for, and probably acceptable to, the researchers, historians, and curriculum specialists to serve in their local instantiations as symbols of their global significance (and so to treat each other and the teachers)—representing global and general actants while serving as local and concrete ones. Their careers are, at least partly, determined by global (national and international) contexts and by general, theoretical, and academic debates and issues.

But this is much less true of the teachers. These teachers have much less opportunity than the researchers and historians to speak to such global and general issues. Further, local contexts potentially impact on them more seriously than they do on the researchers, university professors, and curriculum specialists. They are, for instance, much less likely to move on to a new job in a different state or a new project in a different area.

All these institutional factors, as well as the pervasive presence of cultural and verbal models, like the hierarchy model, together create the social gravity within which words, thoughts, and deeds move and resist. Furthermore, the speaker's dilemma means that Ariel enters a field of implications far in excess of her "private" "intentions."

The problem in action: Relating the actants and hedging

In addition to identifying her actants, Ariel must also verbally express the relationships that hold among them. She accomplishes this through the predicates she uses to relate the noun phrases staging her actants. The significance of Ariel's predicates resides, in large part, in the ways in which these predicates (and the relations they ascribe) are complicit with or contrast with the culture and verbal models available in the context within which Ariel is communicating. We have already argued that in this context, the hierarchical model, with its associated verbal models, is salient.

Note, then, how Ariel's predicates, by and large, contrast with expectations derived from the hierarchical model. Rather than *directing* the project, as the hierarchical model might suggest, Ariel says that she is *taking up* a part (not the whole by herself) or *co-ordinating* (not directing/leading/running) the project. Rather than *leading* the schools, or in any way directing them, she is, merely, *bringing* the two schools together. Ariel is not going to *run* the meetings, rather, she is trying to organise what we are going to do in these meetings. The participants (teachers, researchers, historians, and curriculum people) will not *improve* teaching, teachers, students, or schools, nor will the researchers, historians, and curriculum specialists *help* teachers, as the hierarchical model would suggest—rather these disparate participants will *try to organize* themselves into a cohesive group— *a team.* Finally, the teachers will not be made better teachers by Ariel's efforts, as the hierarchical model would have it, but, rather, the team will get a piece (not a whole) of curriculum up and running and working.

The hierarchical model and the ways in which Ariel lexicalizes the relationships among her actants conflict at many points. The former stresses Ariel as leader and power figure, the latter stresses Ariel as co-ordinator, collaborator, team member. The former stresses causing things to get better, while the latter stresses mutual trying (and possible failing). The former stresses necessary outcomes, the latter claims only that we will know what it *means* to try.

The effect this contrast with the hierarchical model will have on each listener depends, of course, on how the listener thinks and feels about the hierarchical model. If the listener takes it for granted and fails to know it is salient and contested, the listener will find Ariel's sentence "odd" and unexpected, and, perhaps, will find her "weak" and "undirective" (as some did). Listeners who know the model is widely salient and contested will react differently to Ariel's sentence depending on where and how strongly they stand on the attitudes, values, and relationships represented in the hierarchical model.

Of course, Ariel, given her position in the social gravity of the situation, cannot fully avoid some lexicalization of *agency* vis-a-vis the other actants in the meeting and the project—note the string of "I"s that she starts off with, and the fact that "taking up," "co-ordinating," "bringing together," and "organizing" still involve agency and control, no matter how much they attempt to mitigate it and spread it around. However, Ariel uses another device to further mitigate agency and control—with their attendant associations with the hierarchy model: *hedging*.

Hedges are any linguistic device that mitigate the force of a verbal action, whether this be a claim, a question, an apology, a request, or whatever. So, Ariel, instead of saying that she will be taking up the job of co-ordinating the project, says that she will take up only "a part" of the task of co-ordination. She also uses the verb "try" several times. This, of course, is weaker than simply saying that the activities will be done. Finally, Ariel says that the group will get only "a piece" of curriculum (not "a curriculum") "essentially" up and running—where "essentially" hedges just how completely "up and running" this curriculum needs to be (to count as the outcome of these meetings and this project).

While Ariel's hedges mitigate the force of her control and agency, and, thus, too, her possible complicity with the hierarchical model, they have another function as well. Ariel's hedges—especially the "try," "a piece of curriculum," and "essentially"—leave open just to what extent these meetings and this project must actually lead to any issue (result) in the schools or to what extent this result—whatever it is—must be "successful" or "complete." Trying *may* be enough; *essentially* working might be "barely" working or "almost" working.

Ariel's hedges reflect another aspect of multiple coding. The research project Ariel is initiating is interested in studying the social and linguistic interaction of teachers, historians, and curriculum specialists attempting to mount a curriculum (whether anything significant results or not) because it is, in part, devoted to research on language and interaction.

Thus, no matter what these people do or do not accomplish, it will be *data*. The research institute *was* interested, too, in studying the actual curriculum that got produced, as well as its educational effects on the children, but the point is that if this did not happen it would not have wasted the researchers' time or fully frustrated their goals.

We can see this problematic in the actual step by step progression of Ariel's sentence. She says "I'm sort of taking up...trying to *look at how*...," which, indeed, reflects one of Ariel's roles as a researcher, namely to "look at" (research) the others do what they do. But, yet, one can hardly announce this as a goal for the group as a whole, nor can one have the group simply *stimulate* their activities. So, Ariel switches to talk about "what we are going to do in these meetings." However, she then turns to "what it means" for a group of teachers, researchers, and historians to engage in curriculum development and implementation, where the "meaning" (rather than the doing) of this is the primary interest of the research institute, but not the primary interest of anyone else at the meeting (with the possible exception of the curriculum specialists, who worked for, and talked with, the staff at the research institute).

Ariel is, thus, herself multiply coded: she is at the meeting as one of the team (a collaborative researcher bringing the knowledge of research to aid the curriculum development and implementation effort) and one of the researchers who will study the interaction of the team (including herself as team member). Furthermore, the "project" is multiply coded: it is an effort to do something which ought to have "results" that benefit the participants, as well as local students and schools; and, it is, in fact, something that will be researched almost as if it was a laboratory simulation of talk and interaction.

Here we reach the root issue we saw above in the multiple coding of the actants in Ariel's sentence, but with a bit of a new twist: The project and the participants in it were simultaneously "real actants" (out of the "world") and "simulated" ones (in the research space). What they did, in a sense, could just as well have been a simulation—it's just that the best way to get a "realistic" simulation is to have people "really" do something. There is, then, also, a very real conflict between Ariel's de-agentive and collaborative vocabulary and the social gravity of the situation she is in. And, again, the speaker's dilemma leaves her looking more complicit with this social gravity than she wants to be.

The problem and the solution

Multiple coding ensures that there is rarely a single, definitive meaning present in anything said or done, in any object, or in any space of social interaction, and rarely, too, any single and definitive identity for any person present. The speaker's dilemma ensures that the speaker is often as much (sometimes more) a listener and discoverer of her own meaning as any other participant, and therefore not *author*-itative. Social gravity ensures that speakers and listeners are not only *agents* of their words, interpretations, and deeds, but *patients* of the socio-historical forces acting upon them.

But, unfortunately, social gravity, multiple coding, and the speaker's dilemma are "invisible." We all act as if they do not exist. Our everyday "folk theory" of communication—a theory, unfortunately, largely replicated, albeit in fancier language, by modern linguistics and psychology—is that meaning resides *inside* people's heads (Gee, 1992). This folk theory encourages people to project the difficulties and complexities to which social gravity, multiple coding, and the speaker's dilemma give rise—some of which we have surveyed above for Ariel—*into* people's insides, their bodies, minds, and souls: The project failed—or didn't work as well as hoped—*because* of hidden agendas, greed, self-interest, pettiness, jealousy, lack of competence or intelligence, laziness, ill will, poor training, bad attitudes, and so on through a long, long list.

In the end, who and what benefits by these internal attributions—so tempting, yet so wrong-headed (note my internal attribution!) given the workings of social gravity, multiple coding, and the speaker's dilemma? The *status quo*, those in power, the current hierarchy—"Things *can't be changed,*" and "*That's* just the way people just are"—as certainly happened in the project we have just discussed. When the enemy is our oppressor, we must fight back, and that is what any coherent political critical literacy is about. But *here* the "enemy" is *us*, our language, and our theories, which often play right into the hands of our oppressors. In encounters like the one we have been discussing, everyone, in a sense, loses, but those at the bottom of the "information food chain" lose most.

However, the problem helps to delineate the solution: a socially perceptive literacy. A socially perceptive literacy would first and foremost project meaning and "intentions" *outward* onto the social, cultural, and political world. We would mitigate the speaker's dilemma by seeing ourselves as listeners and discoverers, in context, of our own meanings (and analysts of it when distanced from the context). We would mitigate the force of social gravity by studying and understanding—in historical context, crucially—Discourses, the cultural models on which they are built, and the multiple identities to which they give rise. We would all, in the end—at least in institutional settings—have to become both do-ers and analysts of our social words and deeds. Socially perceptive literacy, then, turns out to be a species of "applied linguistics," of "discourse analysis," really of "Discourse analysis." But most certainly not of any sort yet fully realized in theory, practice and pedagogy (though there are bits and pieces, from many different fields, and lots of people starting on the project). And, too, most certainly not any sort that will be ensconced in some academic specialty at the top of the "information food chain"—it must be available to all if we are to fight back against the colonization of the "life world" (Callinicos, 1990; Habermas, 1987) that specialty Discourses have carried out (often with the explicit benefit of the workings of social gravity, multiple coding, and the speaker's dilemma).

Ariel's project—if built on socially perceptive literacy—would have had to go much slower. The participants would have had to form a new discourse (and ultimately Discourse) community and come, too, to understand the potential affects of social gravity, the speaker's dilemma, and multiple coding on their enterprise. They would have to study their own interaction, and come to understand how the Discourse grid of their community and the wider society served as an interpretive framework for them to recognize each other and their words and deeds. They would have to have been in it for the long haul. *That* would have been—as socially perceptive literacy will usually be—bad for business as usual.

REFERENCES

Altmann, G.T.M. (Ed.). (1990). *Cognitive models of speech processing: Psycholinguistic and computational perspectives.* Cambridge, MA: MIT Press.

Apple, M.W. (1986). *Teachers and texts: A political economy of class and gender relations in education.* London: Routledge & Kegan Paul.

Bauman, Z. (1992). *Intimations of postmodernity.* London: Routledge.

Brazil, D., Coulthard, M., & Johns, C. (1980). *Discourse intonation and language teaching.* London: Longman.

Brown, R.G. (1991). *Schools of thought: How the politics of literacy shape thinking in the classroom.* San Francisco: Jossey-Bass.

Callinicos, A. (1990). *Against postmodernism: A Marxist critique.* New York: St. Martin's Press.

Caplan, D. (1992). *Language: Structure, processing, and disorders.* Cambridge, MA: MIT Press.

Chafe, W.L. (1980). The deployment of consciousness in the production of a narrative. In W.L. Chafe (Ed.), *The pear stories: Cognitive, cultural, and linguistic aspects of narrative production* (pp. 9–50). Norwood, NJ: Ablex.

D'Andrade, R., & Strauss, C. (Eds.). (1992). *Human motives and cultural models.* Cambridge, UK: Cambridge University Press.

Dennett, D.C. (1991). *Consciousness explained.* Boston: Little, Brown.

Dow, P. (1991). *Schoolhouse politics: Lessons from the Sputnik era.* Cambridge, MA: Harvard University Press.

Edelsky, C. (1991).*With literacy and justice for all: Rethinking the social in language and education.* London: Falmer Press.

Elman, J. (1990). Representation and structure in connectionist models. In G.T.M. Altmann (Ed.), *Cognitive models of speech processing* (pp. 345–382). Cambridge, MA: MIT Press.

Ellsworth, E. (1989). Why doesn't this feel empowering? Working through the repressive myths of critical pedagogy, *Harvard Educational Review, 59,* 297–324.

Gee, J.P. (1990). *Social linguistics and literacies: Ideology in Discourses.* London: Falmer Press.

Gee, J.P. (1992). *The social mind: Language, ideology, and social practice.* New York: Bergin & Garvey.

Gee, J.P. (1993). *An introduction to human language: Fundamental concepts in linguistics.* Englewood Cliffs, NJ: Prentice Hall.

Gee, J.P., & Grosjean, F. (1983). Performance structures: A linguistic and psycholinguistic appraisal. *Cognitive Psychology, 15,* 411–458.

Giroux, H. (1992). *Border crossings: Cultural workers and the politics of education.* New York: Routledge.

Grabard, S.R. (Ed.). (1991). *Literacy: An overview by 14 experts.* New York: Hill & Wang.

Grosjean, F., & Gee, J.P. (1987). Prosodic structure and spoken word recognition. *Cognition, 25,* 135–155.

Habermas, J. (1987). *Theory of communicative action. Vol. 2: Lifeworld and system: A critique of functionalist reason.* Trans. by T. McCarthy. Cambridge, UK: Polity Press.

Halliday, M.A.K. (1985). *An introduction to functional grammar.* London: Edward Arnold.

Holland, D., & Quinn, N. (Eds.). (1987). *Cultural models in language and thought.* Cambridge, UK: Cambridge University Press.

Latour, B. (1987). *Science in action.* Cambridge, MA: Harvard University Press.

Levelt, W.J.M. (1989). *Speaking: From intention to articulation.* Cambridge, MA: MIT Press.

Minsky, M. (1985). *The society of mind.* New York: Simon & Schuster.

Moffett, J. (1988). *Storm in the mountains: A case study of censorship, conflict, and consciousness.* Carbondale, IL: Southern Illinois University Press.

Resnick, L.B. (1987). *Education and learning to think.* Washington, DC: National Academy Press.

Rose, M.A. (1991). *The post-modern and the post-industrial: A critical analysis.* Cambridge, UK: Cambridge University Press.

Smyth, J. (1992). Teachers' work and the politics of reflection. *American educational research journal, 29,* 267–300.

Stuckey, J.E. (1991). *The violence of literacy.* Portsmouth, NH: Boynton/Cook.

Walkerdine, V. (1986). Progressive pedagogy and political struggle. *Screen, 13,* 54–60.

Wieder, D.L., & Pratt, S. (1990a). On being a recognizable Indian among Indians. In D. Carbaugh (Ed.), *Cultural communication and intercultural contact* (pp. 45–64). Hillsdale, NJ: Lawrence Erlbaum.

Wieder, D.L., & Pratt, S. (1990b). On the occasioned and situated character of members' questions and answers: Reflections on the question, "Is he or she a real Indian?" In D. Carbaugh (Ed.), *Cultural communication and intercultural contact* (pp. 65–75). Hillsdale, NJ: Lawrence Erlbaum.

Willinsky, J. (1990). *The new literacy: Redefining reading and writing in the schools*. New York: Routledge.

No Single Meaning:
Empowering Students to Construct Socially Critical Readings of the Text

Ann Kempe

In recent years literary theorists have challenged the notion of a single predetermined meaning of the text, the nature of academic literary criticism, and the elite canon of literature which excludes particular world views, values and beliefs. The result has been the emergence of reader response criticism as the current dominant theory for the classroom. But there have been problems in practice, not least the paradox created by regarding any personal response to the text as legitimate when in reality some responses are more highly valued than others. The following comment by a tertiary student indicates how students learn to modify their responses towards dominant readings in order to meet assessment demands:

> We should be able to express our own ideas—but our personal views about what we read aren't really respected. You haven't got an opinion until you've got a degree. You write what people with degrees want. It's a real art.

Such confusions and contradictions are certainly not new and have been well documented elsewhere (Gilbert, 1989, 1990). This student like many others has learned reading practices which take for granted that reading is essentially a process of personal and private discovery. When combined with a view of literature as an unproblematic corpus of texts which mirror reality, these kinds of assumptions which are seldom challenged or made explicit, encourage students to ignore the social and ideological nature of their responses. Mellor, Patterson, and O'Neill (1992:41)

From the *Australian Journal of Language and Literacy*, 16(4), November 1993. Reprinted with permission of the author and the Australian Literacy Educators' Association.

contend that students are encouraged to view their responses as "...personal and individual—yet paradoxically universal—and ideologically neutral." Students are therefore unable to analyse how their responses are shaped by the text, by classroom reading and writing practices and by the wider society and culture. Rather than being able to produce and analyse different readings, many students tend towards passive acceptance of the text and the dominant culture. Yet in a world characterized by conflict, oppression and inequality, students must be given access to a more powerful literacy (or literacies) which requires them to resist textual ideologies and to construct socially critical readings of their texts and their culture. Beyond this, critical literacy demands that people will actively contribute to changing and re-making their culture, with the aim of building a better world in which social justice is not merely an empty slogan. But just how difficult is it to develop alternative approaches which result in a more critical classroom practice? There is a danger that the practices which are adopted might become the new orthodoxy, and that empowerment might simply become acculturation into the dominant ways of reading and writing, particularly given that success in the dominant discourses is likely to ensure success in the education system and the workplace. Furthermore alternative discourses are likely to face difficulties in gaining acceptance since they challenge existing power structures. In the context of these considerations it is important to consider the extent to which students will continue to read the teacher as opposed to constructing their own readings. As Ellsworth (1989:298) asks in her critique of critical pedagogy: "What diversity do we silence in the name of liberatory pedagogy?" There are risks and problems, and no simple solutions. However a teaching practice which draws attention to the workings of power and ideology is more likely to be empowering than one which does not.

Classroom implications

Recent critical theory has also been criticized for failing to adequately address the implications for classroom practice. In terms of criteria upon which to judge particular viewpoints Ellsworth argues that critical pedagogy, "offers only the most abstract decontextualized criteria for choosing one position over another, criteria such as 'reconstructive action', 'radical democracy' and social justice" (Ellsworth, 1989). Recent writers (Gilbert, 1989; Mellor et al., 1992; Morgan, 1989, 1992; Patterson, 1989) have provided very useful accounts of the ways in which post-structuralist theories might be applied in the secondary classroom. However the implications for primary classrooms in particular have not been a major focus in recent literature. Yet the primary school is where deconstructive reading, and experiments with writing must begin. To assume that current whole language and genre-based approaches do not require a critical framework is to underestimate and disempower young students. At present there is a tendency to believe that critical theory is not relevant or is too complex for the primary school. Student teachers for instance, probably because they do not recognize different readings as the product of different cultural histories, often ask, "Why would you want to read all that into a text?" This paper seeks to investigate ways in which primary school students might become aware that readings which contradict their own are legitimate, and that the exploration of how, and in whose interests, various readings are constructed, will empower them to read critically their texts and their world.

Reading gender in a primary classroom

The key ideas in post-structuralist theory were the primary source for developing a unit of work in a year 7 classroom. A detailed account of these theories can be found in Belsey (1980), Eagleton (1983), and Gilbert (1989). Gender was selected partly because it is an issue primary students readily relate to and thus appropriate for introducing them to the ideological nature of their texts and their readings. The classroom teacher and I were also interested in exploring gender because it is often viewed as a peripheral issue rather than an integral part of the curriculum. Student teachers in particular are also inclined to believe, as one student put it, that "gender's been done to death." But gender has not always been examined from a socially critical perspective. A study of language and literature necessarily involves issues of gender and power, and it was hoped that the year 7 students would begin to recognize this relationship. The unit of work was audiotaped and, where appropriate, transcript excerpts will be included.

Objectives of the unit

It was anticipated that as a result of undertaking this unit the students would begin to develop the ability to:

- identify the values inherent in texts and readings, and whose interests these values serve.

• analyse different readings to examine the issues involved in the contradictions between readings.

• challenge taken-for-granted or dominant readings.

• examine how the selective use of language and the structured silences work to position the reader to accept the underlying ideology of the text.

• expose the gaps and silences of readings, their own and others.

• construct socially critical readings of their texts and their culture.

Grouping texts

Having considered the objectives, careful consideration was given to the kinds of texts which would be used. In many respects the table on the next page represents what many teachers do when they gather resources for units of work. The difference is that the texts have been selected so that they can be considered in relation to one another. We wanted to be able to compare and contrast the texts closely in order to highlight their constructedness. Thus it was important to provide both conventional and unconventional texts across a range of genres, from different periods and different ideological perspectives. Morgan (1989) uses the term "text clustering" to describe the process of grouping texts and her account of a unit of work on Ned Kelly is particularly useful in terms of ways in which texts might be juxtaposed to illuminate critical theories.

Teaching strategies

As well as considering which texts to juxtapose and when, an appropriate sequence of learning activities and teaching strategies was determined. The strategies which were employed are not new but they were used in different ways for different purposes. A selection of these is outlined below.

• Compare texts of similar generic structure to investigate how texts position the reader to accept particular ideologies (for example, traditional and modern fairy tales).

• Compare an unconventional text with a conventional text to investigate how this opens up multiple readings (for example, compare *Atalanta's Race* with *Princess Smartypants*).

Grouping texts—gender

Narrative

Stories featuring traditional gender roles and relationships from the *Victorian Readers* and *Endeavour Reading Scheme*.

Stories which offer alternatives to traditional conceptions of gender (e.g., *Willie the Wimp* and *Willie the Champ*).

Fairy tales featuring traditional gender roles and relationships (e.g., *Atalanta's Race, Sleeping Beauty, Snow White, Cinderella*).

Modern fairy tales which challenge patriarchal ideologies (e.g., *Princess Smartypants, The Paperbag Princess*).

Visual

Magazines

Dust jackets

Illustrations from children's books

Comics (e.g., *Blondie*)

Popular television series (e.g., *Neighbours, Home and Away*)

Expository

Newspapers (e.g., feature articles and letters to the editor)

- Determine who is under-represented or misrepresented in the text and analyse the text from this individual's or group's perspective in order to highlight omissions and distortions (for example, the roles and relationships given to girls in reading scheme material).
- Make predictions at various points in the text to examine how prior knowledge and assumptions (literary and cultural) influence the construction of readings (for example, predicting the ending to *Princess Smartypants*).
- Add or delete words, phrases, character descriptions or events to challenge the apparent unity of the text and make visible its gaps, silences and contradictions (for example, rewriting stories from outdated readers).
- Construct alternative endings in order to challenge dominant readings and develop an awareness that endings are not natural or fixed but constructed and alterable (for example, write and discuss possible endings to *Atalanta's Race*).

- Use visual forms of representation such as tables, diagrams and drawing to encourage students to become aware that there are alternative ways of interpreting texts which can be used to highlight their constructedness (for example, drawing the typical princess and contrasting this with *Princess Smartypants*).

The successful implementation of these kinds of strategies is dependent upon the use of appropriate questions. This was not an easy task since those old questions such as "What is the author trying to say?" and "What is this character like?" were inclined to come to us more easily than deconstructive questions. We therefore spent some time planning the questions we would ask. These included:

- "What are you thinking about, or feeling while you are reading? How are these thoughts and feelings influenced by your background, your experiences and other texts you have read?"
- "What is the text asking you to think or feel? Do you agree with the point of view offered by the text? Why or why not?"
- "What events or points of view might have been left out of the text? Would you have left them out? Why or why not? Which of the other readings in your class do you feel least or most comfortable with? Why?"

It was anticipated that the use of these kinds of questions, which were adapted to suit the students and the unit of work we were implementing, would encourage the students to develop an increased awareness of their own reading practices. In particular we hoped that students would begin to recognize that their responses to texts are not merely personal but are constructed out of their particular cultural contexts.

Reading magazine texts

The unit began with activities centred around magazine texts. The intention was to focus on the language and visual images used to portray women and men in different kinds of magazines such as *Dolly* and *Women's Weekly*. Different groups were allocated different magazines and the students cut out pictures, words and phrases and placed these on posters. When the children were asked to consider why women and men are portrayed in particular ways it became apparent that for some children these texts reflected reality. One student suggested, "That's just the way things are. That's how men and women are." Here the value of grouping texts became evident because while the posters displayed similarities there were also significant differences which enabled development of the post-structuralist idea that texts construct particular interested versions of reality. We posed questions such as "What view of women/men does this particular magazine promote? How is this different from the views constructed in other magazines? Why is it different? Do you agree/disagree with the images presented? Why/Why not?" Some of the children began to analyse the magazines critically and in several instances indicated what was at stake in particular versions of femininity and masculinity:

> "Magazines like *Dolly* influence girls to think they should be pretty and beautiful and delicate because they want you to buy things."

> "Society expects women to be thin. You might buy their magazines if you think they're going to tell you how to be thin."

> "Anyone should be able to be a builder. It's mainly the society that gives the image that only men should be builders. It's not easy to be different from what society expects."

Comments such as these represent the beginnings of an awareness between language, ideology and power. While these children could certainly not articulate a theory of textuality they are beginning to put this theory into practice. With increased maturity and further experiences with texts they are likely to be able to make the theory explicit.

The "ideal" female/male

Having begun to examine the gendered constructions of femininity and masculinity in magazine texts the students were able to tabulate the characteristics of the "ideal" female and male.

We then discussed whether students would be comfortable applying these terms to the opposite sex. This led to a consideration of the connotations of particular words and how language works to construct particular versions of femininity and masculinity. The use of visual representation for this activity allowed children to become more aware of the way in which binary oppositions (male/female, husband/wife) work to construct and exaggerate differences, thereby playing down or ignoring similarities.

We then read the class the text *Willie the Wimp* in which the central character is the antithesis of the "ideal" male. In this story the mock heroic

"Perfect" female		"Perfect" male	
blonde	blue eyes	hunk	muscular
cute	slim	physical	strong
beautiful	nice clothes	active	witty
understanding	caring	rich	healthy
nice manners	wise	drives a Porsche	mature
tanned	good legs	career-minded	sporty

Willie embarks on a program of diet and exercise so that he will no longer be considered a wimp. While the students empathized with Willie and acknowledged that boys should not have to behave in traditionally masculine ways, in general the boys indicated that they would not behave similarly. Kennard (1986) suggests that readers may engage in a polar reading of the text in which they put themselves into the character's position while they are reading the story but afterwards they use the experience to indicate that they are different. This is evident in the following extract:

T: So most of you felt sorry for Willie. Would you behave like he did?

S: No way!

T: Are there things at school or outside school that happen, that make you feel like this?

S: At school if you were like Willie you'd be called a "woosy."

T: What's a "woosy"?

S: Someone who's not into sport and that kind of stuff and they're—you know a bit weak.

T: So is it mainly what other people expect that influences you to think like this?

S: Yeah, I guess so.

T: All right. What are some of the ways people expect you to behave?

What is also interesting about the above transcript excerpt is the role of the teacher in mediating student responses. The student's last response is somewhat hesitant but the teacher chose to ignore or was unaware of this, perhaps because she was more concerned with getting across her own ideas as opposed to extending those of the students. Because of the power and authority relations which operate in the classrooms the student may have felt obliged to agree with the teacher. Recent research has focused on the role of the teacher as a mediator between the text and the reader, suggesting that the teacher provides a "running meta-textual commentary" which students use to process the text (Luke, 1989). Baker and Freebody (1989) have taken this up and focused on the connections between talk around the text and relations of power and authority between teachers and students. Further examination of this research and its classroom implications is outside the scope of this paper but any endeavour to produce critical reading and writing practices must address these issues.

Having analysed a text which sets out to challenge the notion of the "ideal" male, the students were in a better position to examine how they positioned themselves according to societal expectations, in particular the extent to which their ideas and behaviour reflected a concern to fit the "ideal." At this stage we also used the survey we had conducted prior to introducing the unit to demonstrate how the students' values and beliefs about gender affected their readings of texts. We endeavoured to make this discussion less threatening by collating the results of the survey and converting them to percentages. One aspect we analysed was the fact that with the exception of "washing dishes" (73%) and "helping my mother around the house" (63%), the survey indicated that boys were unlikely to move outside traditional roles, and we discussed how this was consistent with their views of Willie and the suburban gorillas who teased and ridiculed him. It was noteworthy that some of the boys read from a position outside the ideology of *Willie the Wimp* suggesting that the suburban gorillas' viewpoint had been overlooked: "We'd put them in the story more to make you understand them, like you understand Willie."

Re-reading readers

We began by reading the students a piece of text from the *Victorian Readers*:

THE TWINS

"Look-and-Say" words	every	often	high
	would	watch	
"Sound and Say" words	oy		toy
	Roy	Joyce	enjoy
	boy	a-hoy	

1 Roy and Joyce are twins.
They are just six years old and live down by the sea.

2 Every day, their father goes out in his boat to catch fish.

3 They often help him to load his boat.

4 One day father took them with him.

5 Roy took his toy ship and let it sail near his father's big boat.

6 He tied a string to it, so that it would not float away.

7 "Ship ahoy!" he cried out, as he gave a tug to the string and made his ship sail back to him.

8 The twins like to watch the sea-gulls, as they fly near the waves and then high up in the sky.

9 When Roy is a big boy, he will help his father to catch fish in a net.

10 He will be a sailor when he is a man. He likes the sea.

This text proved useful for investigating the post-structuralist idea that the text can never be a single coherent unity. The students readily identified who was ignored, what was not said, and suggested "It doesn't say what the girl was doing," "The mother isn't in the story," and "What about the girl's future?" When they were asked to consider what views of women and men were being suggested by these gaps and silences their comments included: "Males are better," "Males are more active" and "Women aren't meant to be sailors." We were able to demonstrate that these views were not explicitly stated in the text, rather the text positions the reader to bring certain assumptions about gender roles and relationships to the text. Furthermore the students recognized that the readings available to us were different from those available when the text was written:

T: Why do you think the text was written in this way?

S: It's out of an old reader.

T: Yes, good. What difference does that make?

S: That's how they would have thought in those days.

T: What would people in those days have thought about the views of gender in the text?

S: Agree with it probably.

T: Why don't we agree with it?

S: It's different now. Women are allowed to do more things.

The students then examined an extract from an Endeavour reader titled *Fishing with Jim* and were asked to make comparisons between the texts. They realized that while both texts constructed gendered subject positions there were significant differences: "She hasn't been left out in this story but she doesn't do much." The students also identified similarities and differences in the format of the texts. Here we were making use of what Reid (1992) describes as circumtextual framing which refers to the boundaries around the text. In particular we discussed how the format of the text reflected certain views of gender, reading, and education in general. For instance other titles in both the readers suggested patriarchal ideologies. As would be expected this was more pronounced in the *Victorian Reader*. Thus, the juxtaposition of the two texts allowed us to explore another key idea in post-structuralist theory, that there can be no single meaning of the text put there by the author, because the values and beliefs reflected in texts are a product of different historical, social and textual contexts.

At this point the students were asked to rewrite the extract from the Endeavour reader so that it reflected a different viewpoint. It is significant that while the students rewrote the text providing more activities for the girls, the characters remained essentially gendered constructs. For instance girls were nearly always cast in helper roles, boys were the leaders, Mum was there, but Dad was the authority figure. It was apparent that the students believed that gender issues could be resolved by giving equal representation to females and males. We wanted them to go beyond content analysis to a consideration of more complex questions such as the typical boy/girl coupling in basal readers and the fact that males assume responsibility for decision-making except in the domestic sphere. It seems likely that there was a developmental factor involved here, that equal representation was a necessary precursor to forming more critical insights. Subsequent discussion of the students' writing encouraged them to consider how the practices contained in the Endeavour readers had positioned them to accept binary oppositions. We then considered how their texts might be constructed to move outside these oppositions.

The final piece of text used from the Victorian readers was titled *Atalanta's Race*, the story of a princess who "although she was only a girl" could race all the boys. The students readily identified the gendered aspects of language in this text and one of the students commented that the magazine activity had made her see things she would not normally have noticed. For this student the grouping of texts was proving useful because she had begun to realize how the reading of one text influences the reading of subsequent texts (Morgan, 1989). Through discussing responses we endeavoured to demonstrate to other students how their recent experiences with gendered texts might have influenced their predictions and their reading of *Atalanta's Race*. For instance the students did not read "although she was only a girl" unproblematically, nor the events which followed. In the story the prince must win the race not only in order to marry the princess but to prevent his own death. One of the students commented:

> It gave you this image that the prince was like this dream man and to have him die would be disastrous. If he didn't have to die it wouldn't matter so much who won. In a way it's like those other readers, saying girls aren't as good as boys.

At the very least this student is aware of the way in which the text is being constructed to make a particular conclusion seem inevitable. *Atalanta's* race proved to be a very useful example of a closed text. When it came to predicting the ending of the story the students' predictions were quite varied. Some of the students predicted the inevitable, that the prince would win because the story was following the familiar conventions of the fairy tale genre. Other students suggested that different conclusions, while less likely, were possible:

> "She won't stop by to pick up the apple because she wants to win the race." "They tie." "She wins but she tells her father she wants to marry this guy and he mustn't die."

These students were recognising that readings other than the dominant one could be constructed. This activity led to a discussion of what would need to be changed in the text to challenge genre and gender expectations, and make these conclusions more likely.

Princess Smartypants

Having read *Atalanta's Race* and some other traditional fairy stories featuring princes and princesses the students formed small groups and made a list of the language and generic features characteristic of these texts. This was not for the purpose of students producing texts which would rigidly adhere to the fairy tale genre. On the contrary these lists were used as a reference when the students examined what was conventional and unconventional in modern fairy tales. It was hoped that through exploring alternative practices and unconventional fairy stories which invited them to question gender differences, students would be encouraged to write subversive texts. They began by writing and illustrating a description of a princess and then inverted this to provide a description of a princess called *Smartypants*. The activity served as a useful precursor to identifying the incongruous words and images in the text itself, for example the way the visual images of the princess's pets do not fit with the usual connotations of the words. The students were also encouraged to examine the plot devices employed in *Princess Smartypants*. They recognized that the text employs the same plot device as the traditional tales (the prince must commit certain deeds in order to marry the princess) but for different purposes. In *Princess Smartypants* the plot device is employed to disrupt dominant patriarchal discourses, demonstrating that the traditional polarisation of gender roles and relationships in society in general, and the discourse patterning evident in the expectations for princes and princesses in fairy tales in particular, is not inevitable. Once again the students' predictions for the ending were revealing. We had read the story up to the point where the princess gives the prince a magic kiss:

S: She turns him to a frog.

T: Why do you think that will happen?

S: Because there's a fairy story where there is a frog.

T: Yes, is there anything else that makes you think that?

S: It was a magic kiss.

T: Right, fairy tales often make use of magical powers don't they. What will happen after she turns him into a frog?

S: She won't have to get married to him.

T: Why do you think the author might have chosen that kind of ending?

S: Because she's trying to show you don't have to get married to be happy.

Here it is evident that intertextuality is influencing responses. The students have drawn on stories such as *The Frog Prince* and *Sleeping Beauty* and recognized why the text will depart from the traditional ending. Once it would have been sufficient to simply ask why the author might have ended the story in a particular way but we wanted the students to consider all the different ways of reading the alterations to the conventional story. Building on the students' reply to our initial question we asked the class to divide into pairs and write down possibilities. This was useful for demonstrating the plurality of meanings because the students' responses were quite diverse ranging from ideas such as:

"make you think about the ending and stereotypes"
"show that you should do what you want to do"
"make you enjoy the story"
"make the story more modern"
"so you compare the story with other fairy tales"

Princess Smartypants also proved useful for challenging the idea that meanings are purely personal. The students did not each produce a different reading of the character of Princess Smartypants. However there were several readings which arose out of the values and beliefs of different groups. For instance girls generally interpreted Princess Smartypants in a positive way:

"She's a fun person."
"She's showing that girls are clever."

In contrast one group of boys in particular perceived the princess negatively:

"She wants her own way."
"She's trying to get them (the princes) to marry her."
"She's selfish."
"It's lucky they didn't have to marry her."

The boys expected that they would have different attitudes about the story compared with the girls but they were inclined to believe that the difference in their responses occurred simply because girls and boys are by nature different rather than recognising that their differing responses are a product of different social relations and discursive practices.

The text of *Princess Smartypants* constructs an alternative reading position to the traditional view of what it is to be female or male but the boys have rejected this reading. We would have to acknowledge that the boys were resisting the ideology of this text, but many of us would want to challenge their reading. On what grounds can we object to the boys' reading of the text? Operating from critical theory we could not argue that the boys' responses are incorrect. However we would want to demonstrate ways in which responses which reflect patriarchal ideologies work to silence or marginalize the values and interest of women and girls, and thus to sustain existing power relations. But we would also acknowledge that a feminist reading is inevitably a partial interested view. The difference between a pedagogy that operates from critical theory and one that does not, is that the former seeks to make its ideology explicit and to explore ways in which deficiencies and contradictions in current knowledge and assumptions might be addressed. It was therefore appropriate to ask the class to consider all the possible readings of *Princess Smartypants* as opposed to simply stating what they thought or felt she was like. It was also important to ask the students to consider what in their background influenced them to respond as they did and why the boys' and girls' responses differed. Through posing these kinds of questions it was hoped that students might be less inclined to view their readings (and the texts and reading practices which promote such readings) as common sense or natural. However it is also important to be sensitive to the fact that some students come from environments where patriarchal ideologies are firmly entrenched. There is a very real risk that these students will feel alienated and patronized if we allow our own ideological investments to remain unexamined.

From reading to writing

The writing produced by the students when they were asked to write a modern fairy tale demonstrated that they were beginning to experiment in their writing. We had assumed that the children would write narratives and most of them did, but there were exceptions, a poem and a song, indicating that these students were willing to move outside the generic conventions of the fairy tale to experiment with a different form. The piece of text below, written by two girls, is representative of what was produced, unremarkable perhaps but certainly an attempt to construct a feminist position. In particular these students have gained understandings of the traditional expectations of girls in relation to marriage, and perhaps to living happily ever after, and they have chosen to subvert this ideology in their conclusion:

> *Rindercella and her bike*
> Rindercella loved to ride her bike
> She would ride it day and night

She would show it to her kind step sisters
And ride like crazy 'til she got blisters
She always showed it off to the boys
As if it were a precious toy
All the boys would beg on their knees
Will you, will you marry me?
Only if you'll heal my blister sores
And for evermore I'll surely be yours...
Or will I?

It is also noteworthy that Rindercella is both active and assertive, the antithesis of the princess stereotype. The extent to which these students might have begun to move beyond the male-female dualism in their own lives was outside the scope of this study but therein lies the challenge. Davies (1989:137) suggests that we must "learn to think and desire not in terms of the male-female dualism but in terms of the existing variety and complexity of subject positions available to persons." And this is possible only through the development of alternative discourses which legitimize these subject positions. Clearly the same can be argued for difference on other dimensions: black/white, middle class/working class and so forth.

Reflections and implications for future practice

Critical reading and writing were beginning to develop in this classroom but it was very much a beginning and there were a number of areas where changes and improvements might be made in the future. Grouping the texts had been useful for investigating key ideas in poststructuralist theory, and the students appeared to enjoy the range of materials and the opportunity to explore the intertextuality of these texts. However throughout the unit the extent to which our own ideologies and agendas influenced the students' responses was a major concern. After all we selected the texts and determined how they would be used. Furthermore we were accustomed to being the final arbiters of knowledge, and students were accustomed to seeing us in this light. For some students it was somewhat disconcerting to find that there was no one correct meaning of the text which the teacher or the text determined.

In the future it would be important to find ways of minimising the role of the teacher as the source of authoritative knowledge. This could be achieved through an increased focus on learning with the teacher assuming the role of facilitator. The aim would be to build a community of learners engaged in the pursuit of knowledge, while holding knowledge up to constant critical reflection. It would be necessary to refine our questions but more importantly to give the students the opportunity to pose their own. Similarly other strategies which are more learner-centered would be employed. These might include increased use of small group work, and activities such as role play, mime and visual representation. Transcripts could also be analysed by both students and teachers, for the purpose of examining classroom practices, and the relations of power and authority inherent in these.

Although our strategies may go some way towards addressing our concerns, differential power and authority relations will tend to persist. Students will continue to look to us for our versions of text and some may believe that their readings will be more acceptable if they are consistent with ours. And is it possible for us to avoid guiding students towards our reading position? For example are we able to accept a patriarchal reading from our students? We might think we are, but the gaps and silences in our discussions may contradict our invitations to construct different readings. However if we deconstruct our teaching practices and make explicit to students the theory underlying these practices, and if students understand exactly why they are engaging in particular activities and what is being achieved, they will be in a position to make informed choices. Students who are aware that there are choices to be made, that there is no one natural or common sense way of reading their texts and their world, will have more textual and cultural power than would otherwise be the case.

REFERENCES

Baker, C., & Freebody, P. (1989) *Children's first school books.* Oxford: Basil Blackwell.

Baker, C., & Freebody, P. (1989). Talk around text: Constructions of textual and teacher authority in classroom discourse. In A. Luke, S. de Castell, & C. Luke (Eds.), *Authority and criticism on the school textbook.* London: Falmer.

Belsey, C. (1980). *Critical practice.* London: Methuen.

Browne, A. (1984). *Willie the wimp.* London: Little Mammoth.

Cole, B. (1986). *Princess Smartypants.* London: Collins.

Davies, B. (1989) *Frogs and snails and feminist tales.* Sydney: Allen and Unwin.

Eagleton, T. (1982). *Literary theory: An introduction.* Oxford: Basil Blackwell.

Ellsworth, E. (1980). *Fishing with Jim.* Brisbane: Jacaranda.

Ellsworth, E. (1989). Why doesn't this feel empowering? Working through the repressive myths of critical pedagogy. *Harvard Educational Review, 59*(3), 297–324.

Gilbert, P. (1989). *Writing schooling and deconstruction.* London: Routledge.

Gilbert, P. (1990). Authorising disadvantage: Authorship and creativity in the language classroom. In F. Christie (Ed.), *Literacy for a changing world*. Camberwell, Victoria: A.C.E.R. Press.

Kennard, J. (1986). A theory for lesbian readers. In E. Flynn & P. Schweickart (Eds.), *Gender and reading*. Baltimore: The Johns Hopkins University Press.

Luke, A. (1989). Beyond criticism: The authority of the school textbook. In A. Luke, S. de Castell, & C. Luke (Eds.), *Language authority and criticism: Readings of the school textbook*. London: Falmer.

Mellor, B., O'Neill, M., & Patterson, A. (1992). Re-reading literature teaching. In J. Thomson (Ed.), *Reconstructing literature teaching: New essays on the teaching of literature*. Norwood: Australian Association of the Teaching of English.

Morgan, W. (1991). Deconstructing texts, reconstructing courses for textual literacy. In R. Cormack (Ed.), *Literacy: Making it explicit, making it possible (Selected papers from the 16th Australian Reading Association Conference)*. Carlton South: Australian Reading Association.

Morgan, W. (1992). Changing the face of the body of literature: Deviant writing in the secondary classroom. In J. Thomson (Ed.), *Reconstructing literature teaching: New essays on the teaching of literature*. Norwood: Australian Association for the Teaching of English.

Patterson, A. (1991). Power authority and reader response. In P. Cormack (Ed.), *Literacy: Making it explicit, making it possible (Selected papers from the 16th Australian Reading Association Conference)*. Carlton South: Australian Reading Association.

Reid, I. (1930). *Victorian readers*. Melbourne: Victorian Education Department.

Reid, I. (1991). Remaking literature through narrative. In J. Thomson (Ed.), *Reconstructing literature teaching: New essays on the teaching of literature*. Norwood: Australian Association for the Teaching of English.

The Crediting of Literate Competence in Classroom Talk

Carolyn D. Baker and Peter Freebody

Much recent work on classroom literacy has examined the ways that working with texts through variants of reading and writing pedagogies functions to cast literacy practices into forms compatible with institutional imperatives and preferences. That is, classroom literacies can be seen as being designed "for schooling." Studies in this vein (e.g., Baker & Freebody, 1989a; Cazden, 1981; Michaels, 1985; Scribner & Cole, 1981) have shown how school literacy has centred on talk in classroom games and rituals, and how the mark of the becoming-literate and literate student has been the cultural competence or coincidence of being able to produce "expository talk in contrived situations" (Scribner & Cole, 1981). The importance of acquiring school-endorsed ways of talking about text has also been underlined by Olson and Astington (1990) who held that literacy is more general than scribal competence, rather being "competent to participate in a certain form of discourse, *whether one can read or write or not*" (emphases in original).

In early schooling, where students are not credited with the competence to read words on pages independently, "oral and literate" performances are hard to disentangle. Gee (1990) has extended this point to argue that "the ability to talk about school-based sorts of tasks" is "one way in which Western-style schools empower elites; they sound like they know much more than they do." These are all clear signals that it is the production in student talk of booklike text that is listened for and heard as grounds for early classifications of students as more or less "literate."

With these arguments in mind, it could be suggested that the particular kinds of literate practices selected for use in schools are custom-built for one of the school's major functions—classifying students. The possibility,

From the *Australian Journal of Language and Literacy*, 16(4), November 1993. Reprinted with permission of the authors and the Australian Literacy Educators' Association.

in early schooling, of the translation of the ability, accident, or fortune to "look like a reader" (cf. Cochran-Smith, 1985) and to "sound like a book" into levels or degrees of general academic ability is real. It is also consequential for students, given that much of early schooling is devoted to just these kinds of literacy and language-use exercises.

Other recent commentators (Edelsky, 1991; Myers, 1992) have questioned the connections between school-literate exercises and performances and other kinds of (more "personal," "meaningful" or "functional") literacy activities, used by students not for grades but to get other things done in these commentaries, spaces are sought for students to use literacy in ways that by-pass the grade—or achievement-driven credentialing or the formal acknowledgment and assessment of their literacy by teachers. It is not clear in these writings how such more personally meaningful or student-inspired uses of literacies are expected to transform the power relations in or out of the classroom or the distribution of social goods more generally.

These considerations have led some to wonder whether the teaching and learning of "literacy" understood as an activity-in-itself ("reading" and "writing" used intransitively) is a coherent project at all (see Gee, 1990). Further, they have led some to question whether school-based literacies, despite their formal organisation and accrediting by teachers, are any more or less useful to master or know about than any other (informal) kinds of literacies that students also use (Myers, 1992), and how those relativities might be established.

It would appear highly unlikely that literacies outside those that teachers take themselves to be "teaching" or those that they recognize (hear) as properly "literate" could be made part of formal instruction and assessment packages. This would, at a minimum, be another form of institutional appropriation, turning a private/informal practice with text into another publicly accountable/formal way of doing things with words. There is, simply, no way around the centrality of what teachers listen for and hear in the crediting of students with "literate" competence and in the accrediting of that competence through grades or other forms of formal or informal assessment and evaluation.

Efforts to bypass the institutional relations that organize the literate practices that "count"—for marks, or for other kinds of academic recognition—for example, by supplementing the curriculum with non-assessable activities or by celebrating personally meaningful over contrived classroom activities, are not going to alter the point that students will be credited and credentialed differently according to how well they can match the formal academic literacy curriculum as taught and listened for by teachers.

So the pressure is on teachers to produce "literates" who read like, write like, and sound like school books. Classroom literacies will always be "contrived" to the extent that they are theorized, planned, taught, and evaluated; there is some literacy curriculum or pedagogy in place, and a "classroom" without some version of curriculum or pedagogy seems a contradiction in terms. The issue is not whether school-designed literacies will continue to count (they will), but whether the particular forms that are formally taught and learned in schools will continue to be those that privilege the already literally advantaged. This is a policy issue that extends beyond individual classrooms into curriculum documents and literacy theories.

Another aspect of this issue is the extent to which teachers are aware of the sources and consequences of their classifications of literate competence in curriculum documents and in literacy theory. Curriculum documents and literacy theories provide methods and "rules" for finding students more or less literate within the terms of the curriculum and within the terms of the pedagogy. The recent draft National Performance Profiles and Statement policy documents concerning "levels" of language competence (1992, and since substantially modified), as with any such formalism, are full of such rules in the form of idealized statements about what students can and cannot do with text. Teachers match their students against idealized versions of literacy learners, and in this contest, not everyone can possibly come out best. Teachers, like examiners, are also under pressure to discriminate. In effect, they have to find some students better than others—*hear* them as legitimately different—for crediting and credentialing purposes (cf. Freebody, 1992).

One implication of this is that the texts of literacy curricula and pedagogical theories need to be read for their underlying "rule for hearing or reading" students' productions, and for some sense of how this could translate into the production of differences in value and ultimately merit in classrooms. There cannot be any curriculum or literacy pedagogy that is neutral in respect of these consequences. There has been sufficient critique in recent years of the notion of a single essential "literacy" that it is now incumbent on producers of curricula and pedagogies to explicate which literacies are included and which excluded, and in whose interests those choices have been made.

Another aspect of this issue, closer to home for literacy teachers, is the recognition of the extent to which classroom literacy practices are implicated, by derivation from curricula and theories, in the *production* of difference. This becomes ultimately a part of the production of advantage and disadvantage, success and failure, distinction and indistinction. What teachers credit and what they discredit are provided by, among other things, the authoritative sources they go by—their rules for hearing. Walkerdine's (1984) analysis of the child-centered pedagogy in Britain contains examples of how teachers find themselves as competent or incompetent followers of such rules. Explicating the sources and consequences of these rules, and exploring their possible alternatives, are important broad brush-strokes in any portrait of the critical literacy project.

Another part of the critical literacy project, more by way of fine-detailed sketching of classroom practice, is an appreciation of how the classification of literate competence derives also from the literate cultures of which teachers are practising members. In addition to the educational or literacy theories that overtly underpin classroom practices, teachers hold social theories about more or less valuable, coherent, effective and functional forms of language use (Gee, 1990). These are appreciations and misapplications of difference that arise from the social and cultural origins of teachers' own language communities. Michaels's (1981, 1985) analyses of "hearing the connections in children's oral narratives" shows how teachers who are not familiar with non-mainstream (non-School) literacies and oralities have genuine difficulty in making sense of different kinds of oral and literate productions; they do not know how to bridge the distance between some children's language and the school language they as teachers wish to impart. What this implies is that many children in schools are speaking a primary language that is unavailable to teachers. The translation problem is treated as a cultural, or worse, intellectual problem that the students carry or possess. Thus it is hard for teachers to do the apprenticing that they want to do, because they only speak and hear one language (Gee, 1990).

Thus the differential recognition and crediting of literate and oral competence is a form of classification in relation to some curricular or pedagogical standard and in relation to a school-literate discursive community in which teachers are by definition and unproblematically members, models, and distributors themselves. There are class, cultural, ethnic and gender dimensions at work in this privileged discursive community, and in its consequent privileging of some student productions over others.

Teachers then, are engaged in "classifying" student productions in terms of their match to idealized formulations of literacy or literacy-in-the-making. What this amounts to sociologically is an engagement in the production of social class, gender and ethnic relations through the apparently neutral medium of teaching "language" or a "standard language" or "effective uses of language" or whatever alternative carries the day in the formulation of the curriculum.

The social organization of classroom competence

We turn now to examining and illustrating how the organisation of literacy activities in classrooms works in the social organisation of knowledge and, more specifically, in the social production of classroom competence. How does literacy instruction function to produce educational advantage and disadvantage, and beyond that, to produce economic, cultural and social advantage? Where and how are attempts at apprenticing to school-literate culture done? Where and how are students credited or discredited with membership in the school-literate community?

The contents of literacy activities in classrooms, curriculum documents, assessment procedures, and policies serve to cast literacy practices into forms compatible with institutional imperatives and preferences, as noted above. The literacy classroom is an institutional site, and it is also, inevitably, a political one. How is the literacy classroom political?

The force of much of the substantial body of research conducted over the last decade on classroom talk has been to demonstrate the ways in which teachers model and shape a running "metatextual commentary" that counts as the text of the lesson (Baker & Freebody, 1989b). It is this construction by the teacher of the canonical text of the lesson for which students can later be held accountable for having heard and noted. Further, this construction of the canonical text through classroom talk is at work even when the teacher is using questions, including "open" questions, as much as if she were delivering a lecture. Questioning is a powerful device for directing talk, perhaps even more powerful than a lecture, since students are asked to participate in and legitimate their positioning through questions.

More directly for our purposes here, the literacy classroom can be seen as directing its interests at producing the individual as reader and writer, who presents a "literate-assessable" self—a self displayed as functioning naturally and easily in the closed system of practices that the teacher has designed and enacted in her organisation of literacy activities. Students are interactively positioned to present themselves as engaged in "virtual" tasks—tasks that, for instance are recognizably "exercises" in literacy (cf. Edelsky, 1991), and even further, "exercises" in school literacy. Elsewhere in the curriculum, students engage in literate activity for doing geography, science, and so on. In language and literacy classroom, they engage in literate activity as practice in doing literate activity.

Example 1 shows a transcript taken from a reading lesson about eight weeks into the first year of the students' formal schooling, with their average age about five years. The class contains one student, Zak, who is fully literate, and fully school-literate, thanks to systematic teaching by his parents. In literacy lessons, Zak has taken to cruising, helping the other students, and responding to the teacher's complaints or queries about the other students' efforts. It is clear that part of the teacher's work, as documented by Willes (1983), is to model and establish what counts as successful task completion in the classroom, which may be different from what might count as successful task completion somewhere else. It is also clear that the students display differing degrees of clarity about the point or purpose of a teacher's question and the minimal conditions for an answer in the classroom.

Example 1

241	T	Well, how would you find out where it says *slobby*:
242	Jane	You'd look at *slobby*.
243	T	Well how would you do that?
244	S	Oh.
245	S	It's easy.
246	Jane	Find...find the...find the person, like Zak.
247	T	Yes, that's one way, you could go and ask Zak, because he knows how to write *slobby*. But if Zak is busy, what else could you do?
248	Jane	Look on the board.
249	T	Hmm, where would we look...Christine? No, just stay there and tell me darling. Hmmm? There? Where?
250	Chr	Next to the monster.

(From Freebody & Dwyer, 1992)

There are a number of points that we could make about this extract. First, the student Jane hears the first question in the excerpt as a request to locate a word as if she were a reader (how would one locate the word *slobby?*: one would look at it). The teacher continues to seek evidence of Jane's proposed searching process by asking "how" she would "look" at the word. There could be some particular way of looking implied in this questioning sequence. This is, on the surface, and to a non-participant, a very difficult question, some history of sense-making that provides for this to pass as a reasonable question.

Other students intervene at lines 244 and 245 to show that they know something of what the teacher is after, or that the answer is obvious. Jane still has the floor, however, and her next proposal is that she would find Zak. At this point (line 247) the teacher makes clear that the point of the questioning is not to find a practical solution to a practical problem but a hypothetical (model) solution to a hypothetical (model) problem. The modality of the teacher's questions is the conditional how would, how would, what else could, where would we look. Jane's "look on the board" in line 248 is also insufficient, as the teacher extends the sequence further to ask Christine to state where (on the board?) one would look. The teacher's interest seems to be most centrally in how the students would undertake the process of "looking."

The sequence continues (as reported in Freebody & Dwyer, 1992), and shows further the order of questioning and answering being practised here, articulating minute reasoning practices that constitute learning-to-read.

Example 2

254	T	But how do you know that says *slobby?*
255	C	Because it has /s/
256	T	So does this one
257	C	I know that //
258	T	/s/ so does this one
259	S	Cause 'cause they know 'cause it's got a "b," two b's over there
260	Zak	An a "o"
261	T	Oh, that's a good idea, Zak, yes you can look for some other sounds that you can hear *slo:obby* good boy.

In this second example, a continuation of the sequence shown in Example 1, the teacher's questioning appears to be aimed at getting students to articulate what features of the words would be correct or adequate features for the recognition of the word *slobby*. The word has been located, and now it is being examined for the features that make it recognisably what it is. The question "How do you know that says *slobby?*" is to an outsider perhaps equivalent to asking someone "How do you know that this thing is a bus (or, say, a cat, or a tree)?" Again, there is evidence in the talk the invocation of a local rationality for this kind of display of looking and reasoning practices. From lines 255 to 258 the teacher confirms that Christine's identification of a letter is on the right reasoning track, but /s/ alone is not sufficient because other words also have /s/ in them. Another student offers the two /b's/ as an alternative. Zak, out troubleshooting elsewhere, has by this time entered the fray and clinches the exchange by mentioning another letter /o/ in the target word, for which he is rewarded. In line 261 the teacher praises Zak, but the student who offered the /b's/ has also found "some other sounds that you can hear," that may be distinctive to this word in the list. It was Zak's "good idea" that was publicly credited.

By this time the students have almost spelled out the entire word. It appears that the teacher is interested in the identification of alphabetic features of the word. As well, it appears that the students know that questions like "How do you know that says *slobby?*" are at least a possible invitation to show their alphabetic knowledge. Sequences like this one are designed for such displays of reasoning. The students' displays of literacy-in-the-making consist in successful engagement in sequences like this.

There are two inferences worth drawing from this. First, this is not like an out-of-school reading event in many ways; rather it is a simulation, a for-school reading event. A reader, out of school, *would* likely accomplish the task simply by looking at the word without going into an elaboration of how she looks at it. A non-reader, out of school, *would* likely enlist the aid of a competent reader, if the completion of the task mattered enough. The task enacted by this group is in a "virtual" ecology. This leads to the second inference: the self presented by the student is not one that simply can or cannot read. Rather what is called for is the presentation of a simulated self—as learning-to-read. The students come to articulate themselves according to the teacher's theory of what constitutes a learner looking, with partial knowledge, first for and then at a word. The students, in their offerings of /s/ and /b's/, present, effectively, a version of their practical consciousness for the assessment of the teacher. Even Zak, who is recognized as a reader, joins in the procedure of displaying an acceptable version of the learning process.

The point is not that one of the versions presented for accomplishing this task is better or more real than the other, or that there is available a "real" version to begin with, or even that there is some non-simulated way of performing the task posed by the teacher. For instance and for you, right here and now as you read, locate the word *than* in the previous sentence and describe in some non-theorized and real way how you "found out where it said *than*." In the classroom, everyone present knows that they are engaging in a "real simulation," that elsewhere in the world people do not typically go about asking "How do you know that says, *All Bran?*," but that in classroom literacy lessons, such questions and answers are perfectly normal and rational exercises in their own terms. Heap (1990) has provided a framework for recognising the "local rationality" of reading activities in classrooms or in other sites—how specific practices make sense in specific sites.

We could imagine a sequence similar to the one quoted above in which the teacher has a different theory of early reading pedagogy. Students could, for instance, find themselves in a classroom with a teacher who subscribed to a "whole-word-shape" approach to early decoding.

T   But how do you know that says *slobby?*
S1   Because it has a dip shape at the end.
T   So does this one.
S1   know that / /
T   / / so does this one.
S2   'Cause, 'cause they know 'cause it's got a hump, two humps over there.
S3   An a little dip before them.
T   Oh, that's a good idea Zak, yes you can look for some other shapes that you can see...*Slobby* good boy.

Somewhat more plausibly perhaps, we could imagine exchanges among students and a teacher who holds to a "predict-the-word-from-context" approach:

T   But how do you know that says *slobby?*
S1   Because it has *floppy elephant* after it.
T   So does this one.

S1   know that / /

T   / / so does this one.

S2   'Cause, 'cause they know 'cause over there the snake is saying he's
     fat, and the snake is saying this bit too

S3   And it's in the title and it says that...says the title all the way
     through

T   Oh, that's a good idea, Zak, yes you can look for some other
     places in the story where it says the same thing. *Slo:obby floppy
     elephant*, good boy.

The point is that a significant aspect of how the teacher, and gradually and to differing extents the student, hear the adequacy of an answer
relates to the answer's inflection of the pedagogy that is at work in the particular classroom and that is on display through the teacher's questions
and evaluations. It is at least arguable that comparable processes are at
work, in large part through the written words, in later school years.

The naturalization of such exercises in school literacy entails the naturalization of the differences that teachers hear in the contributions of students. Remember that from outside the "local rationality" of this classroom,
the teacher's questions are difficult. Asking questions like "How would you
recognize a bus if you saw one?" would stop conversation dead in many
other settings. How do we recognize a bus when we see one? Inside the
local rationality of the classroom, literate competence consists in being
able to supply orders of answers that match such orders of question. And
the teacher's hearing, and reception of student answers is for her, and everyone present, a running commentary on how well individual students can
produce articulations of reasoning in respect of such questions. In the brief
sequence presented above, Jane and Christine both receive "yes but" hear-
ings of their attempts to produce those articulations; the student who offered the "two b's" might have been included in the praise to Zak, but it is
Zak's contribution that is accorded most credit in the teacher's pronuncia-
tion with the vowel extended of the target work in line 261: "*slo:obby*." This
is evidence of the point made by Heap (1982) in response to Durkin (1979)
that the organisation of conversational exchanges in classrooms are simultaneously for instruction and for assessment.

Teachers do not rely on formal tests to infer how good students are
at literacy; they hear this competence minute by minute in exchanges like
this one. Where they have to work hard to achieve the required articula-

tion of reasoning, they have found something "missing" in a student's contribution. Others, like Zak, are credited with knowing how to supply, on cue, just the missing pieces—the pieces of the task as strictly defined by the theory informing the pedagogy. Each day students chalk up credits and debits in their literacy competence account.

It is worth continuing to explore the propositions that this classroom literacy is as real and as valid as any other kind, and that it is against this classroom literacy that students' literate competence will be found. There is, in classrooms, no where else that the teacher can find it. Much of the work of displaying and crediting literate competence is done through talk, especially in the earliest years of schooling.

Questions and answers as displays of reasoning

The organization of talk about texts is done in ways that provide for the articulation of reasonings. In this respect teachers appear to use literacy events to bring about and enhance students' familiarity and facility with the codes that govern school–endorsed performances. This is a way of accounting for the efforts teachers will put in to explore minute details of literacy practice, as illustrated in Example 1. Everyone is an overhearing audience to the talk, whether they are the current speakers or not. The teacher, also, is helping to produce through practice, "expository talk in a contrived situation." And through her receptions of students' contributions, she is making clear what "counts" as adequate or not. As Heap put it:

> What counts as reading, procedurally, is whatever parties to a setting are apparently justified in believing to be the case about what reading is, what the skills of reading are, and how well any of the interactants performed...whatever the teacher permits to pass, uninterrupted and apparently unchallenged, as an adequate display of reading skill, counts, procedurally as adequate, until further notice. (1991, 128-129)

This again points to the absolute centrality, for young students in particular, of following the talk that goes on about text in classrooms, and of participating successfully in that talk. There is no other source that students can consult to determine if they are reading or learning to read with local rationality, apart from what they see and hear in the course of actual reading events. What teachers are supplying in the course of their talk about texts includes information (instructions) about how reading should be done, and who is doing it well. How the teacher routinely includes and excludes students' answers is the key to finding out whether an attempt is correct or adequate or not. More than this, for both teacher and student, whether or not answers "work" and are found adequate within the ongoing discourse is the key to determining whether or not the student is learning to read, or learning to read properly. In addition to including or excluding answers, teachers make situated decisions whether or not to pursue or repair incorrect answers or to let them pass (cf. Heap, above). The work that is done with particular answers and with particular students in the course of classroom activity is part of the production of difference in recognized classroom literacy competence.

It cannot be predicted in advance which answers in lessons will generate teachers' efforts to repair or correct answers (Heap, 1990), or when side-sequences of clarification might arise (Campbell, 1993) or how much or what kind of reformulation work teachers will put in with particular students to get the answer right (cf. Frency & MacLure, 1979). Certainly teachers do not go looking for trouble. The achievement of successful lessons seems to be organized around the production of a sequence of right answers, with unacceptable answers often marked but stored within the ongoing talk through the "yes but" move and its equivalents.

In our materials we have nothing approaching the breakdowns noted by Michaels (1985) in teacher efforts to assist non-standard English speaking black children to "sound like books." However any classroom transcript shows the routine, regular management and open passing over of "bumps" in the production of a smooth course of reasoning about a text. The point of group discussion of texts seems to be in part the notion that students will learn from each other's overt successes and failures in finding the right answers at the right times, in showing what "reading" is supposed to sound like. In the course of this public, group activity, some students will be found more competent than others, not only by the teacher but gradually by the other students and by herself, through the teacher's meta-commentary on answers. The teacher's point may be instruction, but the teacher's talk can also be heard as assessment.

The example below is comprised of two sequences from a kindergarten reading lesson:

Example 3

1 T   When you're helping me, ( ) use your nicest voice, so I can understand you. OK? Who is that mumbling? Ready Ron? Put your book down. All right put your eyes on the

		right hand side of the page where there's a little school. Remember it's a preschool? Annette have a look at the words up the top and read us the story.
2	A	This is Tony's school
3	T	Super duper, have a look at Tony's school. What's on the top of the blackboard at Tony's school, James?
4	J	( ) tells you it's a rainy day.
5	T	It tells you it's a rainy day ye:es. But what about right along the top of their blackboard, big voice Kelly?
26	T	Look for books, that's right. All right. The little boy's name is To:ony. Have a look at Tony in the first picture, what's he doing?
7	S	( )
8	T	Elaine?
29	E	Drawing on the blackboard.
30	T	He's drawing on the blackboard but what's he drawing on the blackboard, Nina?
31	N	The day?
32	T	Not the day! I can think of something else Valerie.
33	V	His name?
34	T	He's writing his name. Let's all read it together put your finger up the top.
35	T&S	s((unison, singsong)) Tony…is…writing…his…name.
36	T	Ah goodness me. The next one, what's Tony doing? Have a look at the picture, don't look at the words, see if the picture tells you the story, Anna?

In this sequence, credits have gone to Annette and Valerie, while James and Elaine received inclusive "yes buts" and Nina received a "no." There is some confusion in this lesson whether the students should be consulting words on the page or just the pictures. This is further complicated by the fact that the pictures have words in them. The teacher's meta-commentary includes many features noted in Baker and Freebody (1989b), including a page-by-page or picture-by-picture questioning sequence. As with Examples 1 and 2 above, this sequence also includes a concern with "how to look," in this case in the form of instructions concerning where to put one's eyes and how to consult the text (for instance, pictures not words in line 36). Here again, we see that the local rationality of these reading activities is worked out through the engagement of the students in the tasks of looking, pointing and saying here a substitute for "reading." Luke (1992) has developed the notion of the production of the "body literate" through practises such as this.

Kindergarten teachers' questions are extremely difficult to answer. Just how difficult is shown in the incidence of insufficient or inadequate answers. Like many other teachers of beginning reading, the teacher in Example 3 engages primarily in inclusion strategies, using (what turn out to be) partial answers to extend and diversify the reasoning of the students in relation to the rationality of the story, trying to keep everyone's answer included as far as possible. Participating in such sequences relies on "cultural competence" (Hammersley, 1971)—specifically knowing what the teacher wants in the way of an answer, when, and how much. In early reading sessions teachers show students what, when and how much in the meta-commentary. Therefore, inadequate or insufficient answers are highly productive for the teacher's purpose of elaborating the codes of the local rationality. But too many unacceptable answers could stall the story telling, and put the teacher's competence to ask reasonable questions into doubt. It is likely that this is one of the considerations that informs teachers' on-the-spot decisions about whether or not to pursue a response with a particular student, or to look elsewhere (as in lines 30 to 34 in Example 3).

These analyses show that early literacy talk is a highly complicated course of interaction. The texts look simple and the questions look easy, but they are not if you have to answer them. There is a complete overlap of "learning to read" with "learning the reasoning code" that the teacher uses in formulating questions and designing responses to answers. Throughout the talk there is a search for literate competence or displays of literate competence-in-the-making, at the same time that the code is being elaborated. In the process, students' contributions are heard and responded to differently, and entered differently into the ledger. The classroom talk is apparently everyone's collaborative construction, but through the differential crediting and use of responses, the production of differences in literate competence begins.

The problem of how teachers respond to students who are deemed more or less competent has been studied previously (see for example McDermott, 1976, on different practices with "ability-based" reading groups; Michaels, 1981, 1985 on how teachers work with children's oral narratives). In this paper we have examined the beginnings of the process by which students are credited with producing evidence of school-literacy-in-the-making, by studying some brief extracts from classroom events.

Conclusion

Teachers look for and listen for literate competence all the time. They find it in relation to some standards that have been formally theorized through the curriculum or pedagogical training or assumptions, or that are culturally implicit (Freebody, 1992; Ozolins, 1981). Thus these procedures for the location of "literacy" are always, already in relation to a school-literate discursive community, and in relation to specific readings of specific texts. The analyses presented in this paper might serve as a model for teachers to use in examining audio-tapes or transcripts of their own work with students. Some of the issues and questions that can be addressed in other literacy events, in line with some of the points raised here, are:

- Teachers' questions, no matter how simple or straightforward they may appear, admit of more than one answer.
  — Is there evidence of this from the students' answers?
- Teachers' questions may be heard as courses of instruction in how to read.
  — Does the teacher's talk contain evidence for this?
  — How clear are these courses of instruction?
  — How are particular theories about pedagogy and/or literacy acquisition displayed?
- Teachers' receptions of student answers are used to display preferred courses of reasoning.
  — What is done with inadequate or insufficient answers?
- Teachers' receptions of student answers credit students differently with literacy-in-the-making.
  — Who was credited with what?

Within the local rationality of a particular classroom, the student who participated adequately is credited with the status of membership in the classroom as a *community*. A student who does not so participate calls for different inferences to be drawn about her- or himself—inferences about background, motivation, intelligence, personality, cognitive processing, perceptual styles or deficits, or any of the accounts provided by available theories of literacy and learning. Indeed it is evidence of these inferences in the on-going activities of the classroom that signals visually to the whole class group (including to the student in question) that merit is to be withheld. One of the points of this paper has been to demonstrate that this "adequacy of participation" is not to do with some neutral, real-life task completion or problem solving. Rather it is necessary to do with a student's successful display of precompetence within the theory or the pedagogy preferred on that site by the teacher. It is close attention to the teacher's displays of these reasoning procedures that is called for, not *really* knowing how to read or write.

A similar close attention, therefore, is called for on the part of the researcher or the teacher interested in modifying his or her practice. Heritage (1984) has pointed out that the prime talk in the analysis of social life is to "keep a grip on the primary data"—conversational exchange. Literacy events in classrooms are site-specific but not accidental. They are orderly and rational in the terms of the locality. For our purposes, to understand the ways in which theories, research studies, and curricular and policy innovations in literacy education might relate to literacy education practices entails some principled and systematic view of those practices as they actually occur in classrooms.

REFERENCES

Baker, C.D., & Freebody, P. (1989a). *Children's first school books: Introductions to the culture of literacy.* Oxford: Blackwell and Associates.

Baker, C.D., & Freebody, P. (1989b). Talk around text: Constructions of textual and teacher authority in classroom discourse. In S. de Castell, A. Luke, & C. Luke (Eds.), *Language, authority and criticism: Readings on the school textbook.* London: Falmer Press.

Campbell, R. (1983). *Teaching grammar: An ethnomethodological study of a lesson.* Unpublished paper, School of Early Childhood, Queensland University of Technology, Brisbane.

Cazden, C.B. (1981). Social context of learning to read. In J.T. Guthrie (Ed.), *Comprehension and teaching: Research reviews.* Newark, DE: International Reading Association.

Cochran-Smith, M. (1985). Looking like readers, talking like readers. *Theory into Practice, 14,* 22–31.

Durkin, D. (1979). What classroom observations reveal about reading comprehension instruction, *Reading Research Quarterly, 14,* 481–533.

Edelsky, C. (1991). *With literacy and justice for all: Rethinking the social in language and education.* London: Falmer Press.

Freebody, P. (1992). Inventing cultural-capital distinctions in the assessment of HSC English papers. Coping with inflation in an era of "literacy crisis." In F. Christie (Ed.), *Literacy as social process.* Darwin: Northern Territory University Press.

Freebody, P., & Dwyer, B. (1992, July). *Classroom talk as a learning environment.* Paper presented to the NSW Special Education Annual Conference, Darling Harbour, Sydney.

French, P., & MacLure, M. (1979). Getting the right answer and getting the answer right. *Research in Education, 22,* 1–23.

Gee, J.P. (1990). *Social linguistics and literacies: Ideology in discourse.* London: Falmer Press.

Hammersley, M. (1977). School learning: the cultural resources required by pupils to answer a teacher's question. In P. Woods & M. Hammersley (Eds.), *School experience: Explorations in the sociology of education*. London: Croom Helm.

Heap, J.L. (1990). Applied ethnomethodology: Looking for the local rationality of reading activities. *Human Studies, 13*, 39–72.

Heap, J.L. (1991). A situated perspective on what counts as reading. In C.D. Baker & A. Luke (Eds.), *Towards a critical sociology of reading pedagogy*. Amsterdam/Philadelphia: Benjamins.

Heap, J.L. (1992). Understanding classroom events: A critique of Durkin, with an alternative. *Journal of Reading Behaviour, 14*, 391–411.

Heritage, J. (1984). *Garfinkel and ethnomethodology*. Cambridge: Polity Press.

Luke, A. (1992). The body literate: Discourse and inscription in early literacy training. *Linguistics and education, 4*, 107–129.

McDermott, R.P. (1976). *Kids make sense: An ethnographic account of the international management of success and failure in one first grade classroom*. Unpublished doctoral dissertation, Stanford University, CA.

Michaels, S. (1981). "Sharing time," children's narrative styles and differential access to literacy. *Language in Society, 10*, 432–42.

Michaels, S. (1985). Hearing the connections in children's oral and written discourse. *Journal of Education, 167*, 36–56.

Myers, J. (1992). The social contexts of school and personal literacy. *Reading Research Quarterly, 27*, 297–333.

National Statement/Profiles on English. (1992). Melbourne: Curriculum Corporation.

Olson, D.R., & Astington, J.W. (1990). Talking about text: How literacy contributes to thought. *Journal of Pragmatics, 14*, 705–21.

Ozolins, U. (1981). Victorian HSC examiners' reports: A study of cultural capital. In H. Bannister & L. Johnson (Eds.), *Melbourne working papers 1981*. Parkville, Victoria: Sociology Research Group in Cultural and Educational Studies.

Scribner, S., & Cole, M. (1981). *The psychology of literacy*. Cambridge, MA: Harvard University Press.

Walkerdine, V. (1984). Development psychology and the child-centered pedagogy: The insertion of Piaget into early education. In J. Henriques, W. Hollway, C. Urwin, C. Venn, & V. Walkerdine (Eds.), *Changing the subject: Psychology, social regulations, and subjectivity*. London: Methuen.

Willes, M. (1983). *Children into pupils*. London: Routledge and Kegan Paul.

(Sub)versions: Using Sexist Language Practices to Explore Critical Literacy

Pam Gilbert

In January this year, a Sydney magistrate dismissed charges of malicious damage made against four women who had added text to, or "defaced" (as the police claimed), a lingerie billboard advertisement. In a surprising and—I suspect—unprecedented move in this country, the magistrate, Ms. Pat O'Shane, was quoted in a newspaper report as saying that "the real crime" had actually been perpetrated by the advertisers, whose advertisement featured the text "You'll always feel good in Berlei" above the visual image of a woman in underwear cut in half by a saw wielding magician. The four women had added the words "Even if you're mutilated" above the original Berlei ad, in an attempt to make, as one of the women charged with the offence claimed in a newspaper report, "a feminist political statement subverting the advertising text to raise the awareness of sexist advertising."

In this paper, I want to suggest that an examination of issues associated with this particular and contemporary social incident raises a number of important considerations in any discussion of "critical literacy," both in terms of how we might want to define critical literacy as a concept for the classroom, and in terms of how we might begin to address it at the level of practice. I want to suggest that the incident demonstrates key questions about reading and the making of textual meaning, and about what we have often fairly loosely described as "the social context" of a particular text: the web of discourses within which any text is inextricably entwined, and within which readers and writers of texts are inextricably entwined. More importantly it can demonstrate how language practices associated with the construction of gender can often provide a powerful site for work with critical literacy.

From the *Australian Journal of Language and Literacy*, 16(4), November 1993. Reprinted with permission of the author and the Australian Literacy Educators' Association.

Critical literacy in the classroom

I would argue that if critical literacy is to mean anything of significance to us as educators in the nineties, it has to address the practices by
which words enact social meaning, and the practices by which we, as social subjects are able to make the range of meanings they are able to
make—the repertoires of readings they have access to—and it has to address how these repertoires can be broadened. If literacy in its most basic
sense is about having access to the practices involved in the making and
re-making of textual meaning (about being able to write and to read),
then critical literacy must be about an exploration of those practices in
terms of the social meanings such practices implicitly (and perhaps explicitly) authorize or silence.

But herein lies the crunch. As most educators who have worked with
critical language study in the classroom know only too well, classroom
practices that will engage students with the social context of literacy are
difficult to construct and to enact. The social context of literacy learning
has still, as work by Kress (1985), or Gee (1990), or Luke (1993) amply
demonstrates, some distance to travel in classrooms, because the issues
associated with a "critical" literacy are complex. How, for instance, can
students learn about the social context of language, unless they are able
to experience the impact of actual language practices in contexts that are of
interest and concern to them?

In his study of social linguistics and literacies, Gee draws a distinction
between what he calls "acquisition" and "learning," arguing that a
Discourse—his term for "a socially accepted, association among ways of
using language, of thinking, feeling, believing, valuing, and of acting that
can be used to identify oneself as a member of a socially meaningful group
or 'social network'" (p. 143)—is not mastered through learning. It can only
be mastered by acquisition: by experiencing it in functional settings
through a master-apprentice relationship in a social practice" (p. 154).

A grasp of "critical" literacy—of what I would call the social contex-
tualization of language practices—necessitates a grasp of how language
operates in a social sense. And I would agree with Gee that such understandings are learnt in functional settings and can not be divorced from
social practice. To work with a commitment to *critical* literacy, therefore, will
inevitably necessitate an engagement with the politics of language practices,
and examples from Lankshear (1989), Freebody (1992), and Walkerdine
(1990) have demonstrated what this might reveal in terms of group oppression through ethnicity, socio-economic status, or gender. To explore

the social context of language practices is inevitably to explore the networks of power that are sustained and brought into existence by such practices. It is to explore how language practices are used in powerful social institutions like the state, the school, the law, the family, the church, and how those practices contribute to the maintenance of inequalities and injustices. For teachers, it means engaging with issues that are often controversial, certainly contemporary, and perhaps quite volatile.

So: of what value is the Berlei ad incident in terms of exploring both the complexities of critical literacy, and the possible ways we might work with language and the social in classrooms? I suggest that it raises three key questions which are fundamental to working with critical literacy, and in the remainder of this paper I will address each one. Initially, the incident illustrates the potential of working with "real" texts, "real" social practice, "real" cultural networks and groupings. In this case the text is enmeshed within a range of social attitudes, values, and assumptions about gender relationships a field of social knowledge that, I would argue, all contemporary Australians have access to, albeit in a range of ways and from a number of different positions.

Secondly, it provides a demonstration of how different "readings" or meanings can be made from texts, dependent upon the way in which a reader is positioned in relation to a text. Consequently it offers the possibility of exploring a range of readings and how they have been made, and invites consideration of why one reading has been privileged over another. Finally, the incident also provides compelling evidence of the impossibility of reading in a social vacuum. The meanings that were made of this text were possible, because the readers drew differently upon the cultural context. The original advertising text, and its later graffiti addition, can not be made sense of in terms of just the words and images on the page, as if they had no history or content.

Language practices and social constructions of "femininity" and "masculinity"

Texts that address issues of gender particularly as in this example where the central issue is about male violence to women allow entry to particular social practices, if only implicitly, to at least fifty percent of students. *All* women experience the impact of violence, aggression and domination from men to women. Although they may not be able to name such actions or recognize them as oppression, they have *lived* them.

Young women almost daily encounter verbal and perhaps physical harassment in the playground, on their way to school, in casual employment, at parties. They almost daily encounter magazine and billboard images of women in humiliating poses for the male gaze; television images of women being chased, hunted, attacked, raped; news reportage of horrendous assaults, abductions, rapes and murders of women and girls by single men or groups of men. To actually name these practices and to cluster them together as part of a whole pattern, makes for such an uncomfortable picture of the future for a woman, that most of our female students, not surprisingly, choose not to speak about them. But they *know* them at the level of lived experience.

And so do young men, although in a different way. They know the taunts and jeers that both mock women, and keep young men within narrowly accepted bands of masculinity. "Look at your man!" "Don't be a girl." "You're just an old woman." They know the physical pushing, grabbing, fondling. They know the jokes, the put-downs, the insults. They know the power that comes from being male, and the weakness that comes from being deemed non-male. They know gender relations and the construction of femininity and masculinity at the level of real language and real action.

Texts that specifically look at issues of conflict between the sexes— or look at specific representations of women and men—allow students the opportunity to work with known experience perhaps in different ways. Issues of equity and "a fair go" are easy ones for children to latch on to and support, and there is increasing evidence that quite young children can understand more complex matters like sexist language practices and discriminatory social organisation. They may find such matters upsetting and disturbing, because they represent a challenge to much that has been taken for granted, but they are quite able to see the unfairness or narrowness of events surrounding them, if they have access to a discourse or set of language practices which names inequity and narrowness.

The construction of gender is such a dominating set of social practices in our culture that it provides a rich field of shared experiences for working within the classroom. In addition, as most State Departments of Education move towards policies of social justice and equal employment opportunity, gender equity has become almost an authorized field of inquiry. An examination of sexist language practices in our culture could hardly today be deemed controversial or volatile. On the contrary, it would seem to be a field of investigation that would support much of the thinking behind any text-context language policies, or behind any social context language programs.

Textual meaning and textual authority

However the Berlei ad incident provides more than just an example of the potential of gender relations as a common set of social experiences to draw upon in exploring language practices. While material like this can clearly provide an entry point for many students, it also illustrates key issues about reading and textual authority in a way that makes such meanings accessible.

What does this particular billboard text "mean"? Quite clearly it means different things to the different people involved in the incident. Its meaning depends on who reads it, for what purpose, and in what context. It has no singular, finite and static meaning. And yet as this incident demonstrates well, once a text is loosened from its authorized, legitimated meaning, the conditions of possibility for that authorized meaning become accessible for investigation.

Attempts to tie a text to a single "reading" usually serve the interests of powerful social institutions: institutions which rely upon a tightly controlled set of social practices for their operation. The legitimacy and authority of many of the institutions (like the law, some religions and certain political orthodoxies) depend upon the controlling of social meaning, and the exposure of such practices is surely fair game for the critical literacy classroom. Key questions could then be: whose interests are best served by the single meaning so authorized? Why is it important in particular contexts to *control* meaning, and make other readings appear "wrong," politically motivated or just naive?

In the Berlei incident these issues become foregrounded. The "meaning" of the ad became central to the event. A spokesperson (a woman) from the agency handling the Berlei account offered a reading which we could probably regard as a "dominant" reading: the reading many Australians might make of such an advertisement. The spokesperson claimed that the concept used in the billboard ad was well-recognized as a "clichéd magic trick." It was not, she said, a violent situation.

Like a second ad in the series, in which a woman in her underwear was trapped in the hand of King Kong, the ads claim to have been intended to be harmless, rather off-beat attempts to promote Berlei products. They merely provided, the spokesperson said, images of "women in situations they would not normally find themselves in but still feeling comfortable in Berlei." In this authorized, yet really quite bizarre reading, an association with violence and misogyny for the near-naked woman and the saw is ruled out. Both these elements of the design of the text were to be read as incidental and irrelevant to its function of selling underwear. The graffiti artists were said to have missed the point. They had mis-read the text.

I suggest that the five women graffiti artists were well aware of the authorized reading that would be offered of the Berlei ad—the reading which had made it possible in the first place for the ad to be mounted on a billboard and displayed prominently in a busy urban area in a contemporary Australian city. But they made another reading of the text which undermined its smiling innocuousness and foregrounded instead the mutilation of a partly clothed woman. They resisted the dominant reading which read female semi-nakedness and injury as normal and acceptable in contexts aimed to sell by attracting attention. Instead they read both of those elements as dangerous and unacceptable in a society which has high statistics for male violence to women, while claiming to promote equity, justice, and safety for all of its citizens.

Their argument was that the text could be read differently: that its linking together of a partly clothed woman smiling while she was being sawn in half made unavoidable connections with a vast sadistic pornography industry and an increasing incidence of horrendously violent and misogynist sexual attacks on women. And the surprising and extraordinary feature of this incident was that the magistrate agreed with them. She supported the women: she made a similar reading.

Rather than authorizing the legitimacy of the "populist" or dominant reading of this advertisement—a reading which was only possible if the text was severed from other texts related to the mutilation of women—she supported a "resistant" reading which lined the text up within discourses of violence and misogyny. She read *against* the reading argued for by the advertising agency: she read against an a-political reading. Yet this "reader" was positioned powerfully within the institution of the law as a magistrate, within an institution which relies upon the practice of isolating and tying down a single textual meaning.

I suggest that the reading offered by the magistrate would have been a surprise to the women graffiti artists and to the ad agency.

> Account Director Belinda Fookes said she was "a little surprised" that a judge should be condoning a crime against a paid advertiser.

And it is here that a whole range of issues to do with critical literacy can be considered. What "readings" are commonly made by the judiciary on issues associated with women? Why? And whose interests are supported by such readings? One of the first questions the new nominee for President Bill Clinton's Attorney General post was asked by reporters was if she was a feminist. Are new male appointments to the High Court similarly asked if they are patriarchs or masculinists? The temptation here is to suggest that the history of legal readings indicates that the law has not often been able to read through the lens offered by feminism. It has not been able to read women's oppression; it has not been able to read male violence.

A feminist position provides a reading frame through which to filter various social practices in terms of how they work, and for whom they work. It offers ways through which oppressive, unjust, and violent social practices can be recognized, resisted, and perhaps reduced. There may be no single approach to feminism (and no single "feminism"), but for classrooms, a straight-forward approach which regards gender as a social construction held largely in place by a range of social practices—many of them language practices—is a starting point.

Such an approach provides students with a reading frame through which to make other (subversive?) meanings of many of the social language practices of families, schools and the electronic and print media. Basic practices like learning how to recognize sexist road signs, electronic games, and terms of abuse, or learning how to notice inequitable representation of women and men in books, TV programs, films and magazines, are obvious and relatively easy starting points. Gender is not difficult to read, once students have appropriate reading frames. Then the possibility exists for reading subversively in other areas: for reading against a commonsense, preferred and populist set of meanings and foregrounding unfair, unjust and dangerous practices.

Intertextuality and critical literacy

Reading can then be part of a real attempt to read the social: to make sense of the texts and signs of our culture. It becomes functional, connected, integrated. Once reading is freed of the shackles of locating a singular and authoritative textual meaning, it can instead focus on how meanings are made, and how different readings can be made by different groups of people, for different purposes. This will mean recognising both the positions that readers take up in relation to texts, and the discourses that are brought into play by different readers and different readings. It will mean focussing on the intertextual experiences of readers, and the inter-textual connections between social texts. In the Berlei incident, commercial discourses which justify the display of female flesh as a marketing strategy dominated in the construction of the advertising text. This is not surprising: these are recognisable conventions for that particular text-type. Female bodies have been commonly used as a marketing strategy for the sale of most things: beer, cars, holidays in sunny Queensland, classical music concerts, homes, boats.... I think it highly unlikely that students would be surprised or puzzled by the visual combination of two such disconnected images as a bikini-clad model and a can of car upholstery cleaner in a magazine advertisement. They know the reading expected: they have lived with the social reality of this construction of women through magazines, films, posters, TV shows, newspaper articles, all of their lives. And they have also lived with advertisements that constantly push that association to include discourses of violation to women's bodies. Take, for instance, the challenge recently to the "good clean fun" beer ad which showed a woman's clothing being ripped off by a dog.

However in this particular Berlei advertising incident, the reading which legitimated the use of a partly clothed female body as a commercial marketing strategy, was subverted and challenged. A group of women wanted to provide a social warning that other discourses were implicated and given legitimacy by this particular combination: that the text had other readings, some of which were very dangerous to women. They wanted a connection seen between documented social violence to women and the prevalence of advertising texts which sold products through the display of female flesh in humiliating, demeaning, or dangerous situations.

They wanted other readings of this text freed so that they could be named and recognized. They wanted connections made between this text and other texts which harm women. They wanted to emphasize the impossibility and naivety of arguing that an image of a near-naked woman smiling while she was being sawn in half had nothing to do with social violence against women. They wanted the social context of this text restored.

Conclusions

Contemporary social texts—like this particular one reporting on the actions of a group of women—offer rich possibilities for exploring key language issues.

- How are readings or meanings made of texts?
- Why do people make different or "subversive" readings? How is this possible?
- What is the effect of certain readings upon social action and social life?

In this paper I have suggested that texts associated with the social construction of gender relations provide useful starting points for exploring these issues. Gendered language practices are so obvious, so prevalent, and, I have suggested, so accessible to students—*if* students are introduced to a few fairly simple feminist reading frames. Then the social world starts to look a little different, as even young children are able to recognize.

The social construction of gender through language practices provides an obvious window through which to interrogate the authority of a text, and an obvious window through which to explore how social practices and language practices are entwined. It fairly simply explodes the myth that textual meanings are fixed and determined, and demonstrates how important it is to understand the discursive histories of both readers and writers in the making of textual meanings. Once students are able to read and name sexist practices to (sub)vert dominant and more obvious readings then, I suspect, they can understand the critical dimension to literacy.

REFERENCES

Department of Education, Employment and Training (in press). *The construction of gender at the P–3 level of schooling: Report from a Gender Equity in Curriculum Reform Project.*

Freebody, P. (1990, January). *Inventing cultural-capitalist distinctions in the assessment of HSC papers: Coping with inflation in an era of "literacy crisis."* Paper presented at the Inaugural Australian Systemics Conference on Literacy Social Processes.

Gee, J. (1990). *Social linguistics and literacies.* London: Falmer.

Gilbert, P., & Taylor, S. (1991). *Fashioning the feminine: Girls, popular culture and schooling.* Sydney: Allen and Unwin.

Kress, G. (1985). *Linguistic processes and socio-cultural practice.* Geelong, Victoria: Deakin University Press.

Lankshear, C. (1991). Getting it right is hard: Redressing the politics of literacy in the 1990s. In Australian Reading Association, *Literacy: Making it explicit, making it possible* (ARA Annual Conference Papers), pp. 209–228.

Luke, A. (1993). *The social construction of literacy in the primary school.* Sydney: Macmillan.

Walkerdine, W. (1990). *Schoolgirl fictions.* London: Verso.

Critical Literacy
and Children's Literature:
Exploring the Story of Aladdin

Anne Hanzl

The widespread use of literature across school curricula in recent years has created many opportunities for children to interact with literary texts in a variety of ways, not least of which is that critical analysis and evaluation of the texts from various points of view, now usually described as "critical literacy." In a useful discussion of classroom explorations of critical literacy, Comber (1993: 73–83) demonstrates that it is possible for even quite young children to "become aware that texts are socially constructed artifacts and vehicles for different kinds of reality presentation." As Comber points out, given the opportunity and encouragement, children can reach beyond their initial enjoyment of a story to create "multiple readings" of the text to allow for "disruptive" readings, and to construct "critically social texts."

Even the simplest of children's stories carry messages of various kinds, reflecting in conscious and unconscious ways the background, biases and culture of the author and the illustrator. This has always been so, and cannot be otherwise as no one exists in a cultural vacuum, including authors and illustrators. What is changing, however, is the way those stories are "read" by their young audience given the opportunity. Children are learning that there is no one interpretation of what a story is all about and that even within a small group of readers, there will be many opinions as to an author's real intent.

Children are also learning to recognize bias and stereotyping in text and illustration, especially in relation to gender, race, age, mental or physical impairment, and cultural values in general. There are now strong pressures on

From the *Australian Journal of Language and Literacy*, 16(4), November 1993. Reprinted with permission of the author and the Australian Literacy Educators' Association.

authors, illustrators, editors, and publishers of children's books today to ensure that their stories, information texts, and illustrations, are "politically correct." This, of course, begs the question—"politically correct" on whose terms? Does this mean that the great stories of the past can no longer be read, because by today's standards they are no longer "ideologically sound"?

Thoughtful teachers will encourage children to explore such issues, as well as the fact that a story is not necessarily a good story because it satisfies someone's set of criteria for political correctness. Such teachers will also encourage children's personal responses to literary texts, with these responses demonstrating an awareness on the children's part of the cultural and political attitudes underlying the writing/illustrating of the texts. While it will always be important for teachers to encourage children to evaluate texts critically from various stances, we should never forget the importance of engendering a love of literature and reading in children.

"Aladdin": Exploring the story and its background

A great many children will be seeing the Walt Disney film *Aladdin* during the next year or so, and resourceful teachers will see this as an ideal opportunity to explore the world of "The Arabian Nights" with children. These teachers will encourage children to compare and contrast different literary versions of the story "Aladdin" with the film, to read other stories from "The Arabian Nights," and to find out more about the cultural source of the stories: in other words to apply their critical literacy skills, and in the process discover a rich vein of story from cultural and historical sources many of us know little about—stories which are still being told and retold in various ways.

Following are some ideas for such explorations, together with a list of titles which will be useful for teachers and children in their search. There are many editions of stories from "The Arabian Nights"; some for adults (their original audience), and some for younger readers. Some are books of quality with rich language evoking the cultural background of the stories, with well-researched and beautiful illustrations. The best-known stories from "The Arabian Nights" are also available in cheaper, mass market editions, either as individual stories or story collections, but as one would expect, the quality of the storytelling and illustrations is generally not as good in these editions. Teachers and children should seek them all out, however, decide which they like best and why, and immerse themselves generally in this magical world!

The source of the story "Aladdin"

The story "Aladdin" is usually found in story collections with titles like *Tales from the Arabian Nights* and *One Thousand and One Nights*. Why is the word "Nights" included in these titles? In many of these collections the first story is usually about someone called "Shaharazad" or "Scheherazade." Read one or more of these stories. Why do you think this story comes first? Does this story explain the title *One Thousand and One Nights*?

How many stories are included in full collections of *Tales from the Arabian Nights*? (Approximately 200.) When did these stories first reach Europe? (Early 1700s.) Who first translated these stories from Arabic, and into what language? (Galland/French.) Who was famous for his translation of the tales into English? (Sir Richard Burton, 1885–88.)

The cultural/historical source of "Tales from the Arabian Nights"

Find a map of the world and locate the countries included in the area usually referred to as the Middle East. What are these countries called today? What have these countries been called at different times throughout history?

The stories from "The Arabian Nights" come from the oral tradition. In what language were they first written down? (Arabic.) Where else did the stories come from apart from Arabia? (Persia, India, Mesopotamia, Egypt.) Find out what you can about the history/culture of the Arab peoples in the past and present (e.g., the Incense Road; past trade connections with India, China; the great civilizations, rulers; domestication of the camel, horse; importance of the Arabic language in terms of poetry, religion, trade; Islam, the Holy Koran; different ways of life in the cities, villages, deserts; the influence of Islam on art, design, architecture).

The name of Harun Al-Rashid is mentioned in many of the stories from "The Arabian Nights"—was this man a real person? If so, when did he live, and why is he referred to in these stories?

"Tales from the Arabian Nights"

Which of the stories from "The Arabian Nights" are most well known? ("Aladdin and his Wonderful Lamp"; "Sinbad the Sailor"; "Ali Baba and the Forty Thieves"; "The Flying Horse.") Why is it, do you think, that some tales have become better known than others?

Read as many of "The Arabian Nights" tales as you can. Compile your own collection of your favourite stories from this source. Will you include the most popular stories—why/why not?

What criteria do you think modern compilers/publishers of "The Arabian Nights" tales might use when choosing which stories to include in a collection? (Popularity/accessibility of each story; age of intended audience—these stories were originally intended for adult audiences, and more complete collections include many stories which are very down to earth and bawdy—content/language of story; balance of stories with strong male/female characters; budgetary considerations.)

The story of "Aladdin"—characters/characterization

Who are the main characters in literary versions of this story? Should the genie be considered a "character" in the story? Why/why not? Do these main characters correspond with the main characters in the Walt Disney film version? Why do you think the film version has not included Aladdin's mother in the story?

What qualities do each of the main characters represent? Do all the characters in the story have names? It is common in folk/fairy tales for characters not to have specific names—why is this, do you think? What names are given to the characters in the film? Do you prefer to have the characters with/without names?

In what sense are the characters in the film made to conform with modern ideas/concerns?

The story of "Aladdin"—setting

Where is the story of "Aladdin" set? Is the setting the same in all versions of the story? Some versions are set in China—what connections were there between Arab peoples and China in times past?

Is the cultural setting of the story important to the events in the story?

How important are illustrations in creating the setting/cultural background of various versions of the story? Is it possible to tell to what extent an illustrator has researched the cultural background of the stories? How visually authentic is the film in terms of setting/characterization?

The story of "Aladdin"—themes

What seem to be the main themes of the literary versions of the story? (Those who are pure in heart will triumph over those who are evil; those who are resourceful and enterprising will succeed, even if they come from humble beginnings; true love will find a way through trouble.) Are these the themes of the film version? What contemporary issues/themes are included in the film? ("It's inside that counts"; the freedom to make choices; the importance of being oneself.) Why do you think that these themes were emphasized in the film?

The story of "Aladdin"—content

Construct a chart outlining the main events in various literary versions of the story (include main characters/different settings). Compare this with the main events to be found in the film version.

Which parts of the story (if any) are essentially the same in all versions? Why are such stories different in various ways? Do you think that this story will survive all its retellings? Which elements of the story would you include in your retelling of the story?

The story of "Aladdin"—motifs/terminology

What are the motifs in this story (and in other "Arabian Night" stories) that seem to be culturally specific? (The genie/jinn; the magic lamp; the magic carpet; veiled/forbidden princess.) Find out what you can about such motifs and their importance in the past to Arab peoples.

What motifs are common to other folk/fairy tales that you know? (Three wishes/3 days/3 months; curse; prince/princess/king; poor/humble family; magic ring; palace; precious stones/jewels; feast.)

Are there any terms/names used in some of the retellings of the story that relate to the cultural background of the story? (Sultan; wazir/vizier; scimitar; genie/jinn of the lamp; slave of the ring; Ala-al-din; Mustapha/Mustafa; Princess Badr al-Badur.)

SOME USEFUL REFERENCES FOR EXPLORING THE *TALES FROM THE ARABIAN NIGHTS* AND THE HISTORICAL/CULTURAL BACKGROUND OF THE STORIES

"Aladdin or the Wonderful Lamp." In B. Hayes & R. Ingpen, Folk tales and fables of the world, pp. 90–101. David Bateman, 1987.

Ali Baba and the forty thieves. Illus. M. Early. Walter McVitty Books, 1988.

Al-Saleh, K., Illus. R.N. Salim. *Fabled cities, princes & jinn: Arab myths and legends.* Hodder & Stoughton, 1985.

Arabian nights. Illus. Edmund Dulac. Omega Books, 1907/1985.

Hanzl, A., Comp., Illus. D. Pearson. *The Arabian nights of Scherezade.* Bookshelf/Martin Educational, 1988.

Lang, A., Reteller, Illus. Errol Le Cain. *Aladdin.* Faber & Faber, 1981.

Lawson, C. "The Wonderful Lamp." In I. Shah (Comp.), *World tales: The extraordinary coincidence of stories told in all times in all places* (pp. 172–175), Harcourt Brace & Jovanovich, 1979.

Heide, F.P., & J.H. Gilliland, Illus. T. Lewin. *The day of Ahmed's secret.* Victor Gollancz, 1991, and *Sami and the time of the troubles.* Clarion Books, 1992.

McCaughrean, G. *One thousand and one nights.* OUP, 1982.

Riordan, J., Illus. Victor Ambrus. *Tales from the Arabian nights.* Hodder & Stoughton, 1983.

"Scheherazade." In M. Saxby, Reteller, Illus. R. Ingpen, *The great deeds of heroic women* (pp. 91–96). Millennium, 1990.

Classroom Explorations in Critical Literacy

Barbara Comber

Yeah, your brain would have taken it in, like if you just read that book, another book which is the same story line or something, ah your brain will just take it in unconsciously; and you just read it like, "Oh the mum's staying home and she cooked terrible meals and blah blah blah" that's funny, isn't it? You mightn't take it in, you know, serious; and you wouldn't know that you would and it might come up somewhere else, like you're listening to the radio and you fall asleep and the next day you remember everything that was on the radio and it's stuck in your brain.
—Geraldine

The kids might not understand it then but they might kind of hang around; if kids keep getting messages like that, even if they don't really notice it, you keep reading the books...they still get the messages. It will get stuck in their memory.
—John

These quotations are part of an ongoing conversation that took place in a Year 5, 6, 7 composite class over several weeks. The impetus for the discussions was the teacher's question, "Should we read *Counting on Frank* to little people?" (Clement, 1990). Geraldine and John were part of a classroom literacy culture where their teacher, Josie McKinnon, asked students to consider the kinds of social realities constructed in texts. In this article I describe practices from two classrooms where teachers are exploring versions of critical literacy.

Critical literacy, literacy and empowerment, literacy and justice (Edelsky, 1991), explicit teaching (Delpit, 1988), Garth Boomer's epic teacher (1989), postmodern literacy pedagogy (Bigum & Green, 1992) are key descriptors to launch literacy educators into the nineties. In 1991 the *AJLL* included a feature issue on critical literacy and another focus issue

From the *Australian Journal of Language and Literacy*, 16(1), February 1993. Reprinted with permission of the author and the Australian Literacy Educators' Association.

with this title is planned for later this year. In Brisbane in July 1992 a working conference on critical literacy was held at Griffith University. Increasingly educators are writing about literacy and literacy pedagogy in critical discourses (see, for example, *Discourse* volume 12, number 2).

Tertiary educators are being challenged to develop critical social literacy in their pre-service training of teachers (Christie, 1992). Critiques of process approaches and whole language are multiple and varied as educators rush to join the new critical literacy club (see Comber, 1992). However, as the working conference on critical literacy signalled in its title, what critical literacy is or how it is to be constructed are still very much matters of contestation. That critical literacy remains problematic and changing is perhaps exactly as it should be as long as teachers are part of the debate. We need to document multiple cases of critical literacies developed in different contexts.

My interest is in the ways in which teachers construct different versions of literacy and pedagogies from competing educational discourses. I asked a number of teachers what they understood by the term *critical literacy* and what kinds of classroom practices they thought exemplified critical literacy. One of my colleagues responded by making obvious the multiple definitions that already exist.

> That's a tricky one. I understand it as many things a deliberate attempt to position thinking about curriculum and teaching into a more political context and away from unthinking social reproduction; or a new, higher-order level of response to texts (according to some authors anyway); or a way of reading/writing, e.g. reading against the grain, etc., etc.

Another teacher explained that critical literacy involves both consciousness-raising about the discourses of dominant cultures and taking action to resist, expose, and overturn these discourses. Others recalled the active construction of political literacy among peasants in South American societies.

In this paper I explore critical literacy in two primary school classrooms. My reason for focussing on primary classrooms is twofold. Firstly, much of the most illuminating writing about postmodern and critical literacy perspectives has come from educators working in tertiary and secondary contexts (Lee, 1991; Luke & Gilbert, 1991; Mellor & Patterson, 1991; Morgan, 1992).

While there has been a number of penetrating criticisms of primary school literacy pedagogies (Baker & Freebody, 1989; Luke, 1992; Baker & Davies, 1992; Martin, 1984) there have been few classroom descriptions of possibilities for critical literacy in the early years of schooling. Secondly, I want to question any suggestion that critical literacy is a developmental attainment rather than social practice which may be excluded or deliberately included in early literacy curriculum. I hope that the National English Profile will create possibilities for critical literacy in the early years of schooling and not endorse it only for higher levels.

Critical literacy can take many forms (Comber, 1992). In a selective review of literature, I identified three different principles guiding approaches to critical literacy. In classrooms where a critical literacy position is advocated, teachers:

1. Reposition students as researchers of language;
2. Respect student resistence and explore minority culture constructions of literacy and language use;
3. Problematise classroom and public texts.

The teachers whose work is described here have initiated students into a socially critical approach to literacy by problematising texts. In exploring their practices I want to consider some of the following questions about classroom cultures of critical literacy.

What kinds of conversations will children be having about texts?

Whose voices will be heard in these classrooms?

What kinds of questions will teachers be asking?

What kinds of tasks will teachers be setting?

What kinds of knowledge and representations of reality in texts will be contested?

As a starting point for understanding how teachers can help students to become critical readers I find it useful to refer to Freebody and Luke's (1990) descriptive framework of readers' roles. They explain:

> (A) successful reader in our society needs to develop and sustain the resources to adopt four related roles: code breaker ("how do I crack this?"), text participant ("what does this mean?"), text user ("what do I do with this here and now?"), and the text analyst ("what does all this do to me?").

Freebody and Luke (1990) argue that text analysis is part of what successful readers do along with other roles. In the early years of schooling students learn what it means to read and write successfully in terms of school practices. They need opportunities to take on this text-analysis role from the start, as a part of how our culture defines literacy, not as a special curriculum in the later years of schooling or in media studies.

The decisions authors make in books for children

Jenny O'Brien is a junior primary teacher in a suburban disadvantaged school in South Australia. She is constructing literacy events with her five- to eight-year-old students which are infused with her understanding of critical literacy. In particular she works on problematising the texts which children read and the texts which she reads to the class. Here I consider the literacy events that O'Brien constructs in the classroom and what this offers these students in their first experiences of school literacy.

Drawing on insights from Freebody and Baker (1989), O'Brien changed the kinds of ways she talked about texts in her junior primary classroom and the ways in which she encouraged students to read texts. Instead of asking children what they think of a story or which characters are their favourites or what they like best O'Brien encourages the children to consider the text as a crafted piece in which authors make decisions to represent realities in certain ways. Over several terms children were asked questions such as the following:

What do writers say about girls, boys, mothers and fathers in the books you read?

What do adults think that children like to read about?

O'Brien recorded children's responses to these questions on charts as they read numerous and varied texts. After reading *Counting On Frank* (Clement, 1990) she asked the children the following questions:

If you knew about families only from reading this book what would you know about what mothers do?

What would you know about what fathers do?

Students were asked to look for the constructions of reality depicted in texts. O'Brien emphasised through her questions and tasks that writers and illustrators make decisions about what to portray. They could have depicted other kinds of mothers, teachers, fathers, foxes, boys, girls. Even though many of these children had not yet mastered their roles as code-breakers they were already being invited to participate in a critical literacy curriculum where authors' crafting was not simply admired but also disrupted in terms of the versions of reality that were represented. Children were invited to show how they understood the writers' constructions of characters. For example, across a range of tasks O'Brien asked the children to:

Draw a witch like the one in this story.

Draw a different witch.

Draw the mean characters in this story.

Draw different mean characters.

Draw a different Mrs. Fox helping to save her family. Use speech bubbles and labels to show what she could say and do to save her family.

Draw the farmer as he is shown in the text.

Draw a farmer that Michael Morpurgo could have shown in the book.

Draw and label the sort of father Diana Coles showed the king to be in the novel.

Draw and label a different kind of father the king could be.

O'Brien has developed a simple approach to text analysis with very young students. Listing the tasks here does not do justice to the kinds of talk around text O'Brien made possible, but it does show how the tasks that she set for children prevented texts being taken as neutral or natural representations of the world. It also indicates how even in the earliest days of schooling teachers might create a space for children to interrogate the worlds of books. In emphasising the decisions that writers and illustrators make about what they include and how they depict it she has changed the kinds of discussions that students have about texts.

O'Brien did not reserve this kind of scrutiny for literary works. Recently the children analysed Mother's Day catalogues and junk mail using the following task guidelines for their reading and recording.

Draw and label six presents for mothers you expect to see in Mother's Day catalogues.

Draw and label some presents you wouldn't expect to find in Mother's Day catalogues.

What groups of people get the most out of Mother's Day?

Look through the catalogues. Draw and label six kinds of presents you can find in Mother's Day catalogues.

Draw and label the kinds of people who are shown giving the presents to the mothers.

Draw and label any presents you were surprised to find in Mother's Day catalogues.

Make two lists: how the mothers in the catalogues are like real mothers; how the mothers in the catalogues aren't like real mothers.

Make a new Mother's Day catalogue full of fun things.

This intensive examination of the catalogues offered the children an opportunity to consider a gender cultural event and its connection with marketing and advertising. These young children became conscious that shopkeepers make the most out of Mother's Day. There were labelled drawings of Myer and other major retailers. The children realised who pays for junk mail to be put in their letter boxes and what it is intended to achieve.

In O'Brien's classroom children also have opportunities to make a personal response to stories and to construct their own texts, but they do this aware that all texts are based on decisions about ways of presenting the world. Non-fiction texts are also examined in terms of what kinds of knowledge they present and what kinds of information are missing. The children are invited to discuss the kind of information that writers and publishers believe is appropriate for children to read.

In the literate culture that O'Brien is constructing the teacher's role as a mediator between child-reader and authorial text is altered. The sanctity of author is not preserved or romanticised. Rather the teacher acts as a broker in the children's interests to scrutinise the valued portrayals made. She has changed the kinds of questions she asks, the tasks that count as early literacy, and the readings that are possible. In this classroom children become aware that texts are socially constructed artifacts and vehicles for different kinds of reality presentations. O'Brien works with them to examine the "natural" representations in stories and the versions of knowledge authorised in non-fiction texts.

Allowing multiple reading and negotiating critical feedback

Josie McKinnon teaches in a disadvantaged Catholic primary school in an inner suburban area. Towards the middle of the first term she began to prepare her class for critically reading and evaluating the 1992 shortlisted books for the Children's Book Council of Australia Annual

Awards. She started by having them read some of the nominated picture books that were commended in the 1991 list. She also read them a newspaper article about the shortlisted books for 1992, which pointed out that none of Paul Jennings' books were included on the list. What was valued in the awards was questioned and made problematic.

Because the class operated as learning partners with a junior primary class McKinnon had her students consider the extent to which texts were suitable for reading with that age group. In one session, debate arose about whether *Counting On Frank* (Clement, 1990) should be available in the school. The text depicts a boy who is very knowledgeable about all kinds of mathematical trivia and calculations. His skill eventually wins him a trip to Hawaii. The book is narrated from the point of view of this character. Other characters include the boy's father, a TV addict; his mother, an inconsiderate cook who needs her son to help her do the shopping; and a large dog, who is featured in a number of the illustrations. The mother is shown in only one illustration where she is put with the boring grills she cooks every night! She is missing from the final illustration where the boy, father and dog, complete with dog food, leave for their holidays in Hawaii. The book award judges reviewed this book in the following way (1991):

> Rod Clement's book is a work of inventive and creative originality. His use of mathematical and creative ideas opens up discussions of concepts of space and estimation. The thought processes of the little boy are reproduced very authentically through both text and illustration.... There is a lovely use of dead-pan humour throughout.... (p. 4)

The judges construct a narrator who develops a life of his own. We are even told that the little boy's thought processes are "reproduced authentically." The judges contribute to a response to literature that naturalises the world of the text as a version of reality. The only criticisms made by the judges were of a misspelling not picked up during the proof-reading, and the disadvantages of high gloss paper. No mention was made of the ways in which characters conform to stereotypes.

McKinnon decided to spend time on this text. In particular she asked the students to consider whether it was a book that they would want to share with their learning partners in the junior primary. Conscious of her influence on previous discussions she decided to remove herself from the talk and set up the discussion as a class meeting. Each speaker was nominated by the chairperson, Sarah. In describing this extended literacy event

I include segments of transcript of a class meeting to illustrate the kinds of talking that went on over a period of weeks.

Sarah: The first item on the agenda is *Counting On Frank*.

John: It's a funny book...and if the mother had been in there more and been a nicer person it'd be much better and I think much more enjoyable.

Ellie: I don't think the book should be used in the library because it's kind of s...saying to kids like it's kind of sexist and I don't think that's how the world should look; it should be more non-sexist.

Kelly: Um I don't think this book is very good because the father's always saying, If you've got a brain use it; but then again he's never using his brain in the story or you know he's not, he's sort of making a point, and then sort of, and then not doing it himself.

Mary: It's sort of saying that um fathers just sit around and watching TV and laughing at the house, and mothers cook for them meals and make you go shopping with them and cart the trolley around. It's not very...positive, of mothers.

John: I think that like the kid's really square and it means like if you're smart you're square. It's just putting smart people down cos I mean none of them are dressed or anything like...respectable...like it's a bad attitude to people...saying like it doesn't matter, like it might upset Dad or something.

Geraldine: I think it's saying that only the...like it is a very traditional book and I don't think that's very good, but it's also saying that if you've got a lot of time at home you could calculate it all. I mean I couldn't calculate all that like I couldn't know that 24 dogs would fit in my bedroom or anything and I think it would disappoint the little kids if they couldn't calculate it either.

Quyen: The mother doesn't go on holidays. That's just saying that the mum is just stays home to cook and do the housework.

Ellie: I think the pictures are good the kids might you know think they were really good but I think maybe that they should try and get another message across in the book. It's stupid.

Renee: I think that at the end it's really stupid because it's saying like, "Oh leave mum home, she doesn't mean anything except for cooking and she has to look after us," but it's like the dog is more important and it has to come everywhere and the dog food has to too.

Ann: I reckon that when you first look at the book you think it's funny and it doesn't give that impression afterwards except if you look into it a bit more then you start to see what it's actually saying about parents and their personalities.

Geraldine: Yeh, your brain would have taken it in, like, if you just read the book, another book which is the same storyline or something, ah your brain will just take it in unconsciously; and you just read it like, "Oh, the Mum's staying home and she cooked terrible meals and blah, blah, blah." That's funny, isn't it? You mightn't take it in, you know, serious; and you wouldn't know that you would and it might come up somewhere else, like you're listening to the radio and you fall asleep and the next day you remember everything that was on the radio and it's stuck in your brain....

Josie: Do you mean like sub-conscious messages?

Geraldine: Yeh.

Mark: Well I think um it's OK to read it to little kids because um sort of they, they don't they wouldn't really be able to pick that kind of stuff. They just think it's meant to be funny. Because they're not adults to pick up that kind of stuff yet. It might give them sub-conscious messages but they don't really know a lot...about stuff yet. They're just learning how to talk, well not talk um write and stuff.

Ellie: Um well in one way I mean it is true that some people are still really traditional and I mean that's just maybe someone's life, you know the story of their life.

Mary: What Mark said about the book and how it's a funny story...Even though they think it's a funny story they will actually look at the pictures and say, "My mum cooks food like that," it's boring like in the book.

John: Um what Mark was saying and Geraldine was saying, the kids might not understand it then but they might kind of hang around and.... If kids keep getting messages like that, even if they don't really notice it you're still just if...you keep reading the books...they still get messages, it will get stuck in their memory.

The students in McKinnon's classroom have been asked to make a decision about the appropriateness of a text for their younger co-students. It is not a hypothetical task, but constructed in the social reality of their lives. Their teacher has created a space for different kinds of reading in previous discussions about the ways in which writers construct realities. The students responded to the virtual absence of the mother-character in the text and the putdowns that she receives both obliquely and directly. John also pointed out his problem with the main character, a brainy boy, being square. Some of the students worried that for the younger children it might be difficult to distinguish between the view of families constructed by the narrator and their own lived realities. Different students' readings foreground their problems with each of the main characters. It is not only the treatment of the mother, but the father and son represent different kinds of stereotypes, the lazy dad and the brainy but square son. The students' collaborative re-reading of the text begins to reveal a different kind of story than the one they first laughed at.

At the end of a lengthy series of discussions where students argued for many different readings of the book, the class decided to write to the author to raise some of their unresolved concerns and questions. The discussions that followed about the most appropriate way to critique the published work of a writer led to talk about grammar, wording, tactfulness, layout. What you can say and what you cannot and how you say it, became central questions for a group of volunteers who worked on a draft. The principal became the final editor as the volunteers wanted their letter to go out with the school's name attached, realising it might then be read more seriously than a response from a group of unknown individuals. The principal showed them the changes that needed to be made to their text and explained why these were necessary.

The lengthy discussions that McKinnon allowed, the numerous close re-readings, the question about the suitability of a book for younger children and finally the taking action by writing to the author meant that this group of students began to realise that it was possible to read texts in multiple ways and that it was possible to construct critical feedback. Books and authors could be questioned. This was not always easy. Mark resisted this new approach and argued consistently over a number of discussions that it was taking the book too seriously to treat it in this way and that young children wouldn't even notice anyway. Some discussions reached the point where the teacher felt they were getting onto dangerous ground because they were beginning to explore ethical and moral questions and she was unsure how to proceed. This raises some questions about where teachers' reading of texts fits into a critical literacy curriculum, and what teachers might do with the debates and contradictions that emerge. We need more accounts of the ways in which practitioners deal with these questions.

Creating spaces for critical literacy

Critical literacy needs to be continually redefined in practice. The sketches provided here are limited, in that they can indicate only partially how these teachers are attempting to construct classroom cultures of critical literacy. These glimpses may be useful to practitioners new to this term. The following unfinished list of questions represents my attempt to monitor my own work in terms of the spaces I create for text analysis.

Do I:

- create opportunities for critically reading the media's versions of education, schools, students, teachers and literacy?
- create opportunities for critically reading department of education and Commonwealth policy documents and profiles?
- create space for disruptive readings and multiple readings of set texts?
- demonstrate critical text analysis?
- use metatextual tools to scrutinise the constructed nature of texts?
- research the ways in which critical readers, writers and speakers operate in different contexts?

In thinking about what critical literacy might be like in classroom practices, I keep returning to the question, "If you only knew about literacy from being in this classroom what would you think it was for?"

The development of critical literacy for educators

Over the last year I have searched in our newspapers for articles which present a positive view of schooling, literacy achievement and the work of teachers. However such journalism is rare. Rather recent media headlines include such as the following:

"School system a certified debacle"

"Literacy problems a barrier to output"

"Education chief admits school violence growing"

"Employers slam school training"

"Literacy languishes while the cult 'elitists' linger"

"Young readers, writers just make the grade"

"Literacy test attacked as a stunt anyone can pass"

"SA's school system fails the test of time"

We need to ask how teachers are positioned in these texts and why. If we begin to practise critical literacy on texts which construct the nature and effectiveness of our work it may then follow that we will pursue similar kinds of reading in classrooms. Professional associations might become advocates for the publishing of different kinds of headlines about literacy and education. It is time to practise critical literacy about the profession in the community to present alternative readings of teachers' work in schools.

REFERENCES

Baker, C.D., & Davies, B. (1992). Literacy and gender in early childhood. *Discourse, 12*(2).

Baker, C.D., & Freebody, P. (1989). *Children's first schoolbooks: Introductions to the culture of literacy*. Oxford: Blackwell.

Bigum, C., & Green B. (1992). Technologizing literacy: The dark side of dreaming. *Discourse, 12*(2).

Boomer, G. (September, 1989). Literacy: The epic challenge beyond progressivism. *English in Australia, 89*.

The Children's Book Council of Australia Annual Awards: Judges' Report. (1991). Reprinted in *Reading Time, 35*(3).

Christie, F., & team members. (August, 1991). *Teaching English literacy* (A project of national significance on the preservice preparation of teachers for teaching English literacy). Canberra: Department of Employment, Education and Training.

Clement, R. (1990). *Counting on Frank*. Angus and Robertson.

Comber, B. (1992). Critical literacy: A selective review and discussion of recent literature. *South Australian Educational Leader, 3*(1).

Delpit, L. (1988). The silenced dialogue: Power and pedagogy in educating other people's children. *Harvard Educational Review, 58.*

Edelsky, C. (1991). *With literacy and justice for all: Rethinking the social in language and education.* London: Falmer Press.

Freebody, P., & Luke, A. (1990). Literacies programs: Debates and demands in culture context. *Prospect: Australian Journal of ESL, 5*(3).

Lee, A. (March, 1991). Reading the differences. *English in Australia, 95.*

Luke, A. (1992). Stories of social regulation: The micropolitics of classroom narrative. In B. Green (Ed.), *The insistence of the letter: Literacy and curriculum theorizing.* London: Falmer Press.

Luke, A., & Gilbert, P. (Guest editors). *Discourse* (Special Issue: *Australia Discourses on Literacy*).

Luke, A., & Gilbert, P. (March, 1991). Reading gender in a teacher education program. *English in Australia, 95.*

Martin, J. Types of writing in infants and primary school. In L. Unsworth (Ed.), *Reading, writing and spelling,* Proceedings of the fifth Macarthur Reading and Language Symposium. Sydney: Macarthur Institute of Higher Education.

Mellor, B., & Patterson, A. (March, 1991). Reading character: Reading gender. *English in Australia, 95.*

Morgan, W. (1992). Truth or dare: The challenge to literature in critical theory and textual practice. *Opinion, 21*(2).

Torres Strait Islanders Speak: Building a Model of Critical Literacy

*Stephen van Harskamp-Smith
and Karen van Harskamp-Smith*

For too long Maganiu Mala Kes Buai Giz (Torres Strait Islander People) have been the recipients of an externally imposed and disempowering Kole (non–indigenous) education system. Currently, many people in Maganiu Mala Kes (the Torres Strait Islands) are calling for an education that empowers them and encompasses their particular educational concerns. The advent of different conceptualisations of critical literacy, notably those of Freire and Macedo (1987) and Gee (1990), map complementary possibilities for Maganiu Mala Kes Buai (of the Torres Strait Islands).

Our aim in this article is to document the educational concerns expressed in recent interviews with Maganiu Mala Kes Buai Giz, including community Elders, indigenous teachers currently teaching in Maganiu Mala Kes, representatives of the Torres Strait Islander Regional Education Consultative Committee (hereafter, TSIRECC), and indigenous students. The people interviewed were from both Maganiu Mala Kes and the Australian mainland. We then make the case for a model of critical literacy that both addresses the concerns of Maganiu Mala Kes about the imposition of a Kole curriculum, and provides powerful literate survival skills in English literacy and oracy for Ailan peoples.

Maganiu Mala Kes Buai Giz views of education, culture and language

Maganiu Mala Kes Buai Giz see education as a significant process in their lives. It is viewed not only as one of the most viable points of entry to access to the Kole world of employment and political power, but in

From the *Australian Journal of Language and Literacy*, 17(2), May 1994. Reprinted with permission of the Australian Literacy Educators' Association.

some cases has been envisioned by community peoples as having a significant part to play in the revitalisation and maintenance of traditional culture and language. The main educational concerns and desires expressed revolved around these two issues. Foremost was the fear that the younger generations were losing the "old ways" and the traditional vernacular languages (e.g., Meriam Mer, Kala Lagaw Ya). It was this issue that heralded recent community calls for the development of bilingual/bicultural programs in schools, but within a pedagogical and institutional framework more responsive than the existing Kole curriculum. Secondly, there was a definite emphasis on the perceived value of the acquisition of English literacy and numeracy.

In this way, the agenda of many indigenous peoples entails a resistance to assimilation into a dominant Kole culture that is largely irrelevant and superfluous for many remote communities. There is also resistance to a mainstream language rarely spoken outside of school. Michael Nai (personal communication, 23 Sept., 1993), a teacher on the Central Island of Masig (Yorke Island) comments:

VHS: How much English is spoken outside of school?

Nai: None. Maybe when they go to the medical centre...or there is a visitor coming to the island. Kids don't see a reason to use English outside of school.

The situation for English literacy is similar in Masig: students receive very little daily exposure to writing in any language. This has led to a suggestion by some of the Masig residents for the council to "put up signs in English and KLY [Kala Lagaw Ya] around the shop and public notice boards" (Nai, 23 Sept., 1993), with the aim of revitalising traditional language and supporting a preferred bilingual agenda for local schools. The majority of students are bilingual, entering school speaking a language other than English, usually Ailan Tok (Torres Strait Creole). Yet there are to date no official bilingual/bicultural programs established in any Maganiu Mala Kes Buai schools, despite many communities' expressed interest in such programs (TSIRECC, 1992, p. 2).

Clearly, the community needs to make decisions regarding the aims of such bilingual programs: Will English literacy be the goal? Or vernacular literacy? Or Ailan Tok literacy? It is our position that developing literacy in two languages can encourage not only communicative competence and metalinguistic awareness in the development of the second language (L2), but that this approach can also contribute to the oral L1 becoming more stable in form and more highly valued as a legitimate educational end in itself (Kale, 1990).

Ata Mario Mabo, Meriam Elder and trained linguist, revealed his vision of the future of Meriam Mir, a language spoken generally only by the older generation. There is a fear that historical denigration and suppression of the language could win out unless formal and cohesive steps are taken to address the situation.

> There is a large sign inside the school gate that read "English is the language of the school—Do not use Meriam on school grounds."...When I go back home that sign is going to read "Meriam Mir is the language of the school—Do not use English." (Mabo, personal communication, 23 Sept., 1993)

Disturbed at the status of Meriam Mir in the eyes of youth, Elders are receptive to the development of bilingual/bicultural education in an effort to revitalise the traditional language. Yet at the same time there is acknowledgment that English is the language of dominant Kole culture, a prerequisite for Meriam youth to gain access and power in that culture. Ata Mario Mabo explains:

> English we must know...is the main language Australia and in other parts of the world but Language [Meriam Mir] is important to us because of our identity. It is who we are.

Denna Nona, currently a teacher on the Western island of Badu, offered some insights into the perceived value and role of literacy in English for Maganiu Mala Kes Buai Giz: "Education is a way of getting a good job and to get a good job you need to be able to read and write well in English" (personal communication, 23 Sept., 1993). Ross (personal communication, 9 Sept., 1993), a current student from the Eastern Island of Ugar, supports this view of the functional role of English literacy because he hopes to use it to obtain meaningful employment. For him and for many other youth, the perceived value of English literacy is essentially economic. Many Maganiu Mala Kes Buai Giz, then, view English literacy as of value primarily because of its function in the Kole economic and political world rather than as a means to fulfil creative or cultural expression.

Critical literacy: Implications for Edyukeisen Ailan Stail

English is an imposed colonial language from dominant Kole society. In many ways, it represents a historically oppressive relationship with

Maganiu Mala Kes. If English needs to be taught, then let it be taught without hypocrisy and secrecy: better it be a weapon in the hands of Maganiu Mala Kes Buai Giz than used against them. A possible solution lies in the teaching of English literacy within a bilingual educational program and context—but with a critical orientation. We propose that critical literacy can be a valuable orientation for the Kole curriculum. In what follows, we outline ways that a compatible model of critical literacy can be constructed with Maganiu Mala Kes Buai Giz to create Edyukeisen Ailan Stail.

At the foundation of Paulo Freire's (1972) conceptualisation of literacy and teaching as a political practice is the notion of learning to name the world. On this basis, a model for changing that world can be constructed by minorities through the transformative power of language. Literacy enables an entry into "praxis" or reflective action. Freire did not believe that this "critical consciousness" could be facilitated by traditional forms of "banking" education which position the learner as passive and dependent, as a *tabula rasa* who brings nothing of value to the learning situation. In an observation relevant to the history of Kole education of Maganiu Mala Kes Buai Giz, Freire points out that Western education suppresses "dialogue" and generates a vertical dominant/subordinate opposition between teacher and learner, coloniser and colonised.

In its place, Freire envisioned a situation where a dialogue between learner and "facilitator" develops in a relationship of mutual exchange and respect. In an interesting parallel to Freire's vision of a reciprocal learner/teacher relationship, Ugariam Elder Ata Koiki Williams (personal communication, 6 Nov., 1993) informed us that the Meriam Mir verb "Erwre" is translated as both "to learn" and "to teach." In Maganiu Mala Kes, learning and teaching are viewed as a reflexive, singular process—a significant cultural difference for those Kole educators working with indigenous students.

Freire and Macedo's (1987) definitions of literacy and their views on the use of minority languages are of particular relevance to the educational concerns of Maganiu Mala Kes Buai Giz. Freire insists that literacy can be used both as a tool of oppression and the naturalisation of that oppression:

> ...literacy cannot be viewed as simply the development of skills aimed at acquiring the dominant standard language. This view sustains a notion of ideology that systematically negates rather than makes meaningful the cultural experiences of the subordinate linguistic groups.
> (Freire & Macedo, 1987, p. 142)

Literacy and language use are never a matter of skills. They are never apolitical and acultural. How the dominant language, in this instance Standard Australian English, has been used as a tool of exclusion and oppression needs to be made explicit in historical and contemporary contexts. At one and the same time, Kole educators need to recognise and facilitate the contributions of indigenous communities' cultures and language in the school.

Freire and Macedo's second point sheds light on the uses of the students' own languages within the school. The position of Maganiu Mala Kes Buai Giz is that there is a need for bilingual/bicultural education in schools. Using students' own vernaculars and creoles as languages of instruction is an integral step in those students' critical reappropriation of their own cultures and histories, cultures and histories which have often been whitewashed and decimated by the Kole education system. It is to be hoped that future self-determination in Maganiu Mala Kes, in whatever form it may take, can derive from an emancipatory rather than a neocolonial orientation to education. Development of a critical literacy and pedagogy could contribute significantly to that self-determination.

We have thus far stressed the positive aspects of Freire's models and their compatibility with some Maganiu Mala Kes Buai educational concerns. Yet we also want to voice caution. Freire is a product of his own culture and times, and his education in the European selective tradition and his theological background are evidenced in the almost missionary zeal of his beliefs in the "salvation" to be found in acquiring critical literacy. There is much to recommend the acquisition of critical literacy, but literacy in itself, like education and "truth," is not monolithic or absolute.

Maganiu Mala Kes Buai cultures and society have longstanding oral traditions and practices. In remote island communities, there is very little voluntary literacy in vernacular languages and Ailan Tok. In these settings, literacy remains primarily the domain of the school and consists of a range of formal, artificial genres written in English. A potential problem with Freire's belief in literacy as necessary for critical consciousness is that it runs the risk of severely underestimating the rich expressive and local political capacity of oral traditions (cf. Finegan, 1988). This belief may smack of cultural imperialism to some indigenous peoples.

In all, Freire and Macedo's strengths lie in their acknowledgment of the incorporation of minority students' language/s into the mainstream curriculum and in their vision of learning as a two-way dialogue. The work of Gee (1990) offers a complementary explanation of critical literacy, but one which stresses the mastery of Discourses. Unlike Freire, Gee views literacy as a plural entity; that is, people have access to multiple literacies that operate in different social spheres and vary in status and power. He regards literacy as a "social contested term" which can be used to privilege some groups over others. But the value of literacy lies in its potential to be:

> "liberating" ("powerful") if it can be used as a "meta-language" or a "meta-Discourse."...for the critique of other literacies and the way they constitute us as persons and situate us in society (and thus "liberating literacies" can reconstitute us and resituate us).
> (Gee, 1990, p. 153)

As noted above, we are sceptical of the Freirian argument that any literacy is in and of itself liberating. We favour Gee's definition of literacy as a multiple entity and his position that literacy can be appropriated by people to critique dominant discourses.

By "Discourse," Gee (p. 143) refers to culture-specific ways of acting, speaking, valuing, thinking, writing and feeling within a given context or text. He categorises Discourses into two types: "Primary" and "Secondary." What Gee refers to as a person's Primary Discourse is developed during the process of enculturation within the family and in the localised community. It serves as a template and reference point for that person's later acquisition and learning of other Discourses. Secondary Discourse involves communication with public domains such as schools, workplaces and businesses and develops beyond the Primary Discourse in building upon and extending specialised uses of language.

Hence, Gee's vision of critical literacy is based on access to multiple discourses. He goes on to argue that one can only be "critical" if one has access to multiple discourses, using one (e.g., Maganiu Mala Kes Buai) as a "meta-discourse" to criticise another (e.g., Kole). The power of Gee's explanation is that it flips traditional deficit models of literacy education on their heads. As Ata Mario Mabo pointed out, the conventional view of Kole education has been that the languages and cultural knowledges of Maganiu Mala Kes Buai Giz are disadvantages in the acquisition of mainstream English literacy, to be barred at the "school gate." What Gee suggests is that access to a Primary Discourse other than that of the school (e.g., Maganiu Mala Kes Buai) could be viewed as a strong starting point for building critical literacies.

Practical directions

There are many ways that teachers can incorporate some of the considerations encompassed by Freire and Gee's work to benefit their indigenous students. With the implementation of the Queensland English Language Arts Syllabus, genre approaches to the teaching of English have become common in Maganiu Mala Kes and Far North Queensland schools. Unfortunately, quite often genres are presented to students as if they are culturally neutral structures, rather than deliberate cultural and historical constructions. The kind of critical agenda we have described here would require that students study and understand why and how one genre has more cultural and political status than others in Kole society. Students need to know why it is of benefit to them to learn the newspaper report or the expository essay. This rationale needs to include more than a vague explanation that: "one day this may get you a job." Rather Maganiu Mala Kes Buai Giz students should be learning how press articles and reporting have contributed to their historical oppression. This might entail studying media representations of Maganiu Mala Kes Buai Giz and analysing how media continue to construct them positively, negatively or, usually, not at all.

From this point, teachers need to build with students a meta-language of criticism: a language with which to talk about language. This meta-language may take up and incorporate vernacular and Ailan Tok namings and representations of dominant Kole culture, many of which have evolved historically to express resistance to colonisation and invasion. Analysing newspaper headlines for agency can foreground the power relations in media representation. To talk and write critically about whose interests are being served and how genres and authors construct and position their subjects and readers, students will need a conceptual base which enables them to identify and name "cultures," "racism," "sexism" and so forth. These analyses can provide the basis for classroom "counter-constructions" of genres (Singh, 1989): in this case, the rewriting of newspaper reports from Maganiu Mala Kes Buai cultural and political perspectives.

Any text that indigenous students study can be viewed from a similar critical perspective. The literary canon that indigenous students encounter in English classes exemplifies the Kole curriculum in action. The study of *Hamlet* at Thursday Island High School is a case in point. Shakespeare contributes very little to the everyday lives of Maganiu Mala Kes Buai Giz and introduces students to yet another foreign language. Admittedly, there are difficulties in incorporating Maganiu Mala Kes Buai literature into the curriculum, written in either English or traditional/Creole languages, as very little exists at the secondary school level to date. Our point is that teachers of indigenous languages have to come to an understanding of the cultural/political nature of literacy, and of the problems that arise from the uncritical imposition of Secondary Discourses and a colonialist literary canon.

The reading and writing strategies taught in many schools are not "natural" ways of approaching "normal" everyday tasks—they are, in fact, Kole "ways of doing" valued in the mainstream curriculum. Maganiu Mala Kes Buai students often do not have the prior experience with Kole Secondary Discourses in their homes prior to starting school. Further, as we have argued here, many of them come from homes where vibrant and functional oral practices fulfil diverse and specialised communicative and creative needs in vernacular and/or Ailan Tok. It is important for teachers to understand that while the acquisition of these Kole Secondary Discourses may be desired by and of some economic benefit to indigenous students, the failure to acquire them does not amount to failure in family and community. In many cases, non-acquisition may be an act of resistance on the part of the indigenous student—a valid response that should be acknowledged as such, rather than labelled with derogatory attributes.

A beginning

Ideally, it would be preferable for Maganiu Mala Kes Buai Giz to be able to exercise independent control over the education of their children. This would involve a system which would reconceptualise education in our own image: Edyukeisen Ailan Stail. Presently and pragmatically though, English literacy and oracy have been acknowledged by many communities as required survival skills for Ailan peoples, particularly given the historical and contemporary situation of contact and oppression. Current educational patterns of irrelevance and disempowerment cannot continue. We feel that critical literacies, applied across the curriculum, have the potential to arrest and reconstruct these patterns.

Our interviews with Maganiu Mala Kes Buai Giz make the point that the Kole curriculum—including Western models of critical literacy— needs to be made to adapt and fit Maganiu Mala Kes Buai ways, and not the other way around. Without this, well-intentioned language and literacy initiatives will result in yet another "top-down" imposition, the latest in a long series of colonial interventions. We believe that a critical literacy framework can be revised and attuned to the desires and needs of different Ailan communities and students. Dasol.

REFERENCES

Finegan, R. (1988). *Literacy and orality.* Oxford: Basil Blackwell.

Freire, P. (1972). *Pedagogy of the oppressed.* New York: Herder & Herder.

Freire, P., & Macedo, D. (1987). *Literacy: Reading the word and the world.* South Hadley, MA: Bergin & Garvey.

Gee, J.P. (1990). *Social linguistics and literacies.* London: Falmer Press.

Kale, J. (1990). Controllers or victims? Language and education in the Torres Strait. In R.B. Baldauf & A. Luke (Eds.), *Language planning and education in Australasia and the South Pacific.* Clevedon: Multilingual Matters.

Singh, M. (1989). A counter-hegemonic orientation to literacy in Australia. *Journal of Education, 171*(1), 34–56.

Torres Strait Islander Regional Education Consultative Committee. (1992). *Educational policy for the Torres Strait.* Brisbane: QATSIECC.

Making Community Texts Objects of Study

Allan Luke, Jennifer O'Brien, and Barbara Comber

In varied communities, literary reading and writing are a relatively minor part of people's everyday lives (e.g., Barton & Ivanic, 1991; Heath, 1986). Further, the transfer of training of reading and writing practices from schools to occupational and community life remains a real problem for many students. In response, state curricula have pushed beyond emphases on literature students and personal narrative to include the study of "functional" texts: from job forms and advertisements to instruction booklets and media texts, brochures and invoices.

While many programs now feature these community texts, there is a pressing need for critical ways of working with and talking about texts and their institutional contexts. By "critical" we mean ways that give students tools for weighing and critiquing, analysing and appraising textual techniques and ideologies, values and positions. The key challenge, then, is how to engage students with study of how texts work semiotically and linguistically—while at the same time taking up how texts and their affiliated social institutions work politically to construct and position writers and readers in relations of power and knowledge.

This article explores how community texts can become essentials of critical literacy programs. We begin with a framework for critical literacy, reviewing recent developments in the teaching of community textual resources. We then describe classroom experiments at critically questioning and analysing these texts. The approaches reviewed here are broadly applicable and adaptable, taken from primary, secondary and tertiary classrooms with diverse age groups and students, including ESL, Aboriginal and migrant students.

From the *Australian Journal of Language and Literacy*, 17(2), May 1994. Reprinted with permission of the authors and the Australian Literacy Educators' Association.

From functional to critical literacy

The texts of everyday life are not innocuous, neutral texts requiring simple decoding and response. They are key moments where social identity and power relations are established and negotiated. Consider these examples: toy advertisements construct a world of gendered childhood and then invite the reader into that world as an enthusiastic consumer. Contracts build up legal versions of the world—with actors, possible actions and consequences—and then lock signatories into binding obligations and compliances. Texts and authors thus re/present and construct a version of the social world; and they position or locate the reader in a social relation to the text and to that world. They do so through various linguistic and semiotic techniques.

Many lessons productively teach students to identify and use textual aspects of representation (e.g., "field") and relations (e.g., "tenor"). But in themselves they cannot provide a cultural and political analysis of the text. What is needed are lessons that foreground the social and economic "conditions of production" and "conditions of interpretation" of the text (Fairclough, 1989). That is, students need to be encouraged to research, speculate about and second-guess the institutional agendas, ideologies and human agents behind and at work in the text (conditions of production), and to talk about their and other readers' social standpoints, community projects, cultural resources and positions (conditions of interpretation). *This requires more than a technical analysis of language, but as well a "reading of the cultures" around, behind, underneath, alongside, after and within the text.*

Many approaches to teaching literacy as cognitive processes, linguistic knowledges, or skilled behaviours are suspect for what they *don't* say about the texts and institutions taught. What one learns to be "functional" at, where, how, to what ends, are all loaded decisions that serve interests in the cultural and economic order where one is instructed to "be" functional (Lankshear & Lawler, 1987). In this way, the uncritical teaching of how to read and write the most simple, basic "functional" text supports particular social relations and institutions. When we teach the job application uncritically, we teach one how to "be" or "do" the corporate identity, to see the world as an employee might, and so forth. As Gee (1990) points out, even a medicine bottle label features particular values and positions—a possible world where the reader (as prospective purchaser, medicine consumer and "patient") is constructed and located.

Left uninterrupted, everyday texts play major parts in building and reproducing social structures. Unequal institutional power relations, discriminatory race relations, restrictive versions of gender identities, one-dimensional versions of cultures—*unrecognised as such*—become taken for granted templates that people use for perceiving, classifying and acting upon social reality (Bourdieu, 1992). Critical literacy teaching begins by problematising the cultures and knowledges of the text—putting them up for grabs, for critical debate, for weighing, judging, critiquing (Edelsky, 1993). Learning the linguistic structure of texts can be a crucial part of this process. But a social analysis of texts also requires classroom frames for talking about how and in whose interests social institutions and texts can refract and bend social and natural reality, manipulate and position readers and writers. Such an analysis can also provide the groundwork for "changing the subject" of texts, and for strategically intervening in social contexts.

Two approaches to studying community texts

A valuable approach to the study of community language resources has been developed by Heath and Mangiola (1991). Their orientation towards "viewing language as an instrument and an object of study" (p. 33) is part of a broad agenda for "at risk" U.S. linguistic and cultural minority students. That program includes: cross-age tutoring and analysis of their own participation in cross-age literacy events, and the collection, coding and analysis of community language texts. Spoken texts (e.g., casual service encounters, television broadcasts) were transcribed and analysed for "turns," "setting" and "context" and for specific aspects of dialect, "colloquial" and "formal" style (p. 31). Written texts (e.g., public health brochures, political leaflets, laboratory manuals) were analysed for cohesion, "persuasive language" and so forth. Teachers and students developed coding instruments for discourse analysis, often undertaking several analyses of an audio-taped or transcribed text. Heath and Mangiola report that students developed a new metalanguage for talking about language and literacy, using terms like "research," "data," "evidence," "dialect," "turn taking" and became much more analytically sensitive to language variation and use, their own and that of others. The program also led to increased student interest, motivation and expanded language repertoires. But while it encouraged students to discuss "manipulative language" and to "explain and argue with texts" (p. 41), its emphasis was on "functional performance of transactions in a heavily bureaucratic society" (p. 48). The program lacked an emphasis on the critical social analysis of the texts.

The problem is that teaching students "appropriateness" without an analysis of social institutions and power relations risks disguising those relations as "natural," "the ways things are" and should be (Fairclough, 1992). A student may master particular language forms and "choose" to use them in, for example, a job interview or service encounter. But the very notion of choice implies that s/he knows that there are other options in that encounter, multiple agendas at work in any exchange, other ways of negotiating relationships and structuring information, doing business or establishing identity, and that s/he can see through attempts to constrain her or his options and possibilities.

Unfortunately, a stress on "how language works appropriately" in contexts may stop short of giving learners a critical purchase on how those texts and contexts might be negotiated or reconstructed differently. The danger is that the text—with the weight of an institution behind it (e.g., bank, church, school, business, government)—can come to stand "beyond criticism" (Luke, deCastell, & Luke, 1989). And that learners, especially young and second language learners, are taught an "over-deferent stance towards the text" (Wallace, 1992, p. 61).

Wallace describes an approach that aims to focus tertiary students' attention on conditions of production and reception, as well as on linguistic features. Like Heath and Mangiola, her initial step was to have students collect community texts, including advertisements, letters and newspapers. In small groups, students were instructed to:

1. Try to classify the texts...Suggested categories might be: requests from charities or causes; public information leaflets; professional reading material.
2. When you have worked out five or six broad types of text, try to identify the following:
   a. who produces them? e.g., public bodies, commercial enterprises, local authorities;
   b. for whom are they produced, i.e., who are the consumers or the expected readers of the material?
   c. why has the text been produced?
   d. is this type of interest or relevance to you? why or why not?
   e. choose one text from each category which particularly appeals to you, either because of its style or content and discuss with other members of your group.

(Wallace, 1992, p. 66)

These classification tasks get readers speculating about and building up knowledge about the kinds of social and cultural institutions that generated the texts (a), their target audiences and ideal readers (b), and their political and economic intents and consequences (c). At the same time, the activity sets out to focus readers on their own discourse resources and cultural experiences that can be brought to bear on texts (d), (e). Note that at this stage, their classification of genre is non-technical (1), based on their gist of the text's institutional format and source. This is an important move: the aim is to get students to see the text as an *institutionally located and motivated social strategy* first, rather than as an array of linguistic features.

From there Wallace shifts to a broad content analysis. At this point, readers identify and discuss topics and discourses, author and reader positions, and strategic silences and absences in the text. This composite list of starter questions for interrogating texts draws from Wallace (pp. 71–75) and Luke (1991):

1. What is the topic?
2. How is it being presented? What themes and discourses are being used?
3. Who is writing to whom? Whose voices and positions are being expressed?
4. Whose voices and positions are not being expressed?
5. What is the text trying to do to you?
6. What other ways are there of writing about the topic?
7. What wasn't said about the topic? Why?

These questions can be followed up in whole class, groups or paired activities with specific text analytic tasks. For instance, we have tertiary students generate lists of "wordings" for particular portrayals (e.g., "list key words that refer to Keating or Hewson") or discourses (e.g., "list all the medical terms in this brochure"). Word lists (i.e., lexical classification or semantic network schemes) can be particularly valuable for showing students how texts build up representations and portrayals, and how they often do so in binary oppositions. Working with a recent *Newsweek* article on North Korea, we had students list all of the adjectives and verbs affiliated with North Korea and those with South Korea. Not surprisingly, they discovered a pattern of binary oppositions (e.g., "peaceful," "friendly," "stable" versus "menacing," "dangerous," "shadowy") that favoured the South.

Wallace (1992, pp. 78–79) moves her students on to more detailed work on lexicogrammatical functions and features, including collocations (e.g., "What adjectives or nouns collocate with X?"); agency (e.g., "What/ who initiates an action?"); the use of mood to position the reader (e.g., "Affirmative? Imperative? Interrogative?"); pronouns (e.g., "How does the writer refer to self, subjects and reader?), etc. The aim in these activities, like Heath and Mangiola's, is to build students' analytic resources for examining language at work, but to do so in a way that shows them how texts work *politically* to refract, distort and position.

The achievement of technical understanding is not, in itself, critical literacy. Too often, linguistic analysis and literary deconstruction are treated as instructional ends in themselves, rather than means for socially productive textual work. We would argue that *text analysis and critical reading activities above should lead on to action with and/or against the text.* That is, there is a need to translate text analyses into cultural action, into institutional intervention and community projects. This might involve: rewriting the text, changing its topics, perspectives and portrayals, or drawing upon divergent cultural resources or discourses; writing or speaking to its authors or institutions; developing written or spoken or media revisions or criticisms; further research about the institutions or issues raised by the text; further data collection on community texts and contexts, and so forth (cf. Moll & Greenberg, 1990).

In sum: our approach to making community texts objects of study proceeds in four interconnected actions. Their sequence can vary, but we would argue that all are necessary.

1. Talk about the institutional conditions of production and interpretation.

2. Talk about the textual ideologies and discourses, silences and absences.

3. Discourse analysis of textual and linguistic techniques in relation to 1 and 2.

4. Strategic and tactical action with and/or against the text.

Classroom explorations: Mother's Day catalogues

To discuss these actions further, we describe an approach to critical literacy with community texts undertaken with 5–7-year-olds in a school located in a mixed-race, lower socio-economic area. We begin with Jennifer O'Brien's account of the activities, then turn to a joint commentary and suggestions for further development.

Jennifer O'Brien

Every year junk mail (e.g., from K-Mart, Big W, Target) pours into letterboxes, presenting itself as a source of suggestions about suitable presents for Mother's Day. In 1992, I wanted students to look at these catalogues as texts that create particular versions of reality in order to persuade people to spend money. I wanted them to think about who benefited from the production of these texts and about how they constructed women's lives, and to come up with other possibilities not offered by the text. Each student was given this template to guide their reading, drawing, writing and discussion.

I want to give you a chance to think in new ways about Mother's Day catalogues.

- Draw and label six presents you expect to see in the catalogues and draw and label some presents you wouldn't expect to find.
- Draw and label six kinds of presents you can find in Mother's Day Catalogues.
- What groups of people get the most out of Mother's Day?
- Make two lists: How the mothers in the catalogues are like real mothers and how the mothers in the catalogues aren't like real mothers.
- Draw and label any presents you were surprised to find in the Mother's Day catalogues.
- Draw and label the people who are shown giving the presents to the mothers.
- Make a new Mother's Day catalogue full of fun things instead of clothes and things for the house.

In order to produce lists of "expected" and "unexpected" presents, students had to think about how "mothers" are constructed. They were fascinated by how accurate their predictions had been. To help students clarify "who gets the most out of Mothers' Day," I asked:

- Who produces these catalogues?
- Why are they in your letter box?
- Why do they go to all that trouble just to let you know that these things are available?

The students identified major retailers. They also discovered that the "catalogue mothers" were slim, "well-groomed" and not portrayed in the kinds of contexts and activities that they associated with their own mothers and caregivers. In designing the new catalogues, the students portrayed the mothers and caregivers in different ways: on holidays, enjoying rides in planes, going out to dinner, relaxing, watching movies, and jumping on trampolines.

At the time, I considered the activity successful. Students were given opportunities to consider the conditions for the production of these texts and to identify textual techniques of representation. It also required them to think differently, to construct other kinds of possibilities for mothers. But Mother's Day as a cultural practice was not questioned, nor were issues of race and culture raised. The following year I decided to deal with the catalogues in a more explicitly critical way: to look for the groups of mothers who were not included, and to explore what it meant for the construction of women in "fast capitalist" consumer society.

To do so, in 1993 I began with a series of questions intended to put the taken-for-granted cultural practice of Mothers' Day on the agenda.

- What happens on Mother's Day?
- Why do we have Mother's Day?
- What is Mother's Day for?
- Whose family celebrates Mother's Day?
- Why do we have a special day for mothers?
- What part do these groups of people play in Mother's Day (mothers, children, fathers, grandmothers, teachers, restaurant owners, shopkeepers)?
- What do "fathers" have to do with Mother's Day?
- Where do children get the money to buy presents?
- Where do presents come from?

Students investigated which kinds of women were represented as recipients to presents. They cut out pictures of presents recommended for mothers and categorised them. I then asked the students to write and draw in response to the following questions: According to these catalogues, what sorts of things do mothers like? Here we explored the ways in which textual practices construct gendered identities and produce a limited but purposeful version of what mothers are like and what they do.

We then turned to questions of silence and absence: "Whose mother isn't here?" Students cut and pasted photographs of mothers under headings which included cultural groups in the class. They found that most of the women in the catalogues were young, Anglo-Australian and pretty. They identified Greek, Lebanese, Cambodian, Vietnamese and Aboriginal mothers as missing. This led to a lively and extended discussion about the fact that so many groups of women (including heavy-set and older women) were invisible.

We then developed and administered a written survey so students could collect data on their mothers' and caregivers' attitudes and preferences. This five-item survey included questions on preferred gifts and activities, likes and dislikes. Students documented many trends: that their mothers and caregivers enjoyed and desired many things that weren't in the catalogues, especially rest, leisure, happy family relations and appreciation, and "peace and quiet." The survey also showed that they preferred gifts that didn't turn up in any of the catalogues: horror novels, cats, roller blades, tickets to the movies, Greek food, and photographs. This second round of activities, then, was quite successful in foregrounding the gaps between the constructed worlds of commerce and the students' worlds. The students found that the women's world constructed in the text was narrow, but one among many possibilities and, as importantly, that the catalogue represented only those aspects of women's lives that resulted in consumer spending.

Commentary

The 1992 lessons drew the students' attention to the institutional conditions of production of the texts (i.e., the commercial interests) and those of interpretation (i.e., their own discursive resources and cultural backgrounds). The key theme that emerged was the exclusivity of the representations and portrayals of women and mothers. Questions encouraged students to speculate on who produced the text, with what ends in mind; they also foregrounded the students' differing expectations and sense of what "real mothers" are like. In this regard, these were lessons in the "social construction of motherhood" (Phoenix, Woollett, & Lloyd, 1991). The productive textual outcome was a "rewriting" of the catalogues which foregrounded representations from their own families and communities.

The activities in 1993 extended the analysis to pick up omissions and the interrelationships in gender, class and cultural difference. They also led directly onto further research work that required the design, administration and interpretation of written surveys that redirected students' attention from the text towards action in family and community settings.

These lessons stressed actions 1 and 2 of our template for critical literacy. They could be developed further towards a more detailed discourse analysis of the language features and techniques (3) and towards exploration of further modes of productive cultural action (4). Text analysis with this age group might include the following activities.

1. The building of lexical chains to detail the constructions of "mothering" in the texts (e.g., "words used about mothers"; "words placed near the words or pictures of mothers").

2. Identifying the use of moods (e.g., interrogatives and imperatives to position and direct the consumer).

3. Analysing the semiotics of colour and layout to establish gendered oppositions and identifications.

4. Detailing further the layout and linguistic conventions of questionnaires and surveys.

The rewriting and survey work could lead on to other forms of cultural action with and/or against the text. These might include: interviewing or writing to retail outlets to discuss the findings; oral or video histories of their mothers' lives, cross-cultural data analysis; replicating the project with children's consumer items, and so forth. All would use and extend text types, data collection procedures and critical text analysis.

Reading texts and cultures

Working with community texts has several immediate benefits. First, it directly takes up problems of curriculum relevance and student motivation. Many students—including those most "at risk" in early reading and writing programs—remain unconvinced of the significance of reading and writing in everyday life. Building curriculum around everyday spoken and written texts students themselves gather, research and analyse shows them the inescapability and variety of language in everyday life, and the tangible social and economic payoffs of reading and writing.

Second, an emphasis on everyday texts and language speaks directly to the "transfer of training" problem. Textual practices and analyses of the texts of everyday life can be taken out into the community as soon as they are taught for experimentation, use and transformation. There is no "waiting period" or "leap of faith" required for results and fields of applications. The approaches we have described here have different emphases.

1. *Language awareness*: Programs like Heath and Mangiola's stress ways of reading and ways of writing about language and literate practice. Like many current genre-based programs their aim is to tune up students' eyes and ears to the ubiquitousness of text and discourse, and to how texts work.

2. *Critical literacy*: Our emphasis is on how language and literacy, text and discourse are implicated in the power relations and face-to-face politics of everyday life.

The first emphasis, language awareness, is essential. But to teach the former without the latter is to risk reproducing those power relations as given, as part of a taken-for-granted view of the world. Critical literacy sets out to encourage students to begin to see that literate practice is always morally and politically loaded—and that to work with a text doesn't necessarily involve uncritically buying into its world view or position. Where this is the case, reading a Toyworld catalogue might entail questioning why it was written in the first place, who benefits from the purchase of particular kinds of toys, whether to read it at all, as well as an understanding of its techniques and a reconstruction of its messages. Learning to work with a memo might entail learning how to see through, critique and practically reconstruct a particular corporate agenda.

There is a great deal of work to be done by classroom teachers and teacher educators in building constructive ways of talking critically about texts—vocabularies for discussing power relations, textual knowledge and truth claims, gender and cultural identities. In a heteroglossic democracy, where many readings and voices have the right to be heard and seen, the principle must be that all texts and discourses can be rigorously debated, all forms of difference entertained. Educational access and equity do not just entail a chance to learn how texts work. They require a forum where one is given the opportunity to see and weigh the cultural, gender and social class perspectives, possibilities and options of texts and readings.

REFERENCES

Barton, D., & Ivanic, R. (1991). (Eds). *Writing in the community*. London: Sage.
Bourdieu, P. (1993). *The field of cultural production*. Cambridge: Polity Press.

Edelsky, C. (1993). Education for democracy. Address to the U.S. National Council of Teachers of English Annual Conference, Pittsburgh, PA.

Fairclough, N. (1989). *Language and power.* London, Longman.

Fairclough, N. (1992). (Ed.). *Critical language awareness.* London: Longman.

Gee, J.P. (1990). *Social linguistics and literacies: Ideology in discourses.* London: Falmer Press.

Heath, S.B. (1986). The functions and uses of literacy. In S.C. de Castell, A. Luke, & K. Egan (Eds.), *Literacy, society and schooling.* Cambridge: Cambridge University Press.

Heath, S.B., & Mangiola, L. (1991). *Children of promise: Literate activity in linguistically and culturally diverse classrooms.* Washington, DC: National Education Association.

Lankshear, C., & Lawler, M. (1987). *Literacy, schooling and revolution.* London: Falmer Press.

Luke, A. (1991). Lexical classification. Critical literacy conference workshop materials, Griffith University, Brisbane.

Luke, C., de Castell, S.C., & Luke, A. (1989). Beyond criticism: The authority of the school textbook. In S.C. de Castell, A. Luke, & C. Luke (Eds.), *Language, authority and criticism.* London: Falmer Press.

Moll, L.C., & Greenberg, J.C. (1990). Creating zones of possibilities: Combining social contexts for instruction. In L.C. Moll (Ed.), *Vygotsky and education: Instructional implications and applications of sociohistorical psychology.* Cambridge: Cambridge University Press.

Phoenix, A., Woolett, A., & Lloyd, E. (1991). (Eds.). *Motherhood: Meanings, practices and ideologies.* London: Sage.

Wallace, C. (1992). Critical literacy awareness in the EFL classroom. In N. Fairclough (Ed.), *Critical language awareness.* London: Longman.

"...and What About the Boys?" Re-reading Signs of Masculinities

Grant Webb and Michael Singh

Introduction

Current events are doing much to foreground issues of masculinity. For instance, while the debate over Sydney's Gay and Lesbian Mardi Gras has ranged across a complex array of issues (e.g. economics, religion, party politics and broadcasting), it has also heightened our awareness of different forms of masculinity. On the other hand, the recent publication of Peter Cameron's (1997) book, *Finishing School for Blokes*, has reminded us that some traditional forms of masculinity are still being privileged within educational settings and impinging upon optimal educational outcomes of both males and females at all levels of institutionalised education.

Despite on-going efforts to suppress and marginalise issues of gender, for example by means of direct government intervention on occasions (Lingard, Henry, & Taylor, 1987; McHoul, 1984), they are, for the moment at least, still on the educational agenda. This is largely as a result of the work of the women's movement and a legacy of the support of the former Federal Government. More particularly, women's research and scholarship has provided on-going critical analyses of men and masculinities (e.g. Harding, 1986; Luke & Gore, 1992). Likewise, related scholarship on issues of sexual orientation has also contributed by questioning naturalised notions of sexuality and gender, raising questions, for instance, about homophobia and homo-eroticism in physical education (Griffin, 1989; Griffin & Genasci, 1990). These developments have led to the questioning of prevailing forms of masculinities, forms which can now be regarded as potentially changeable.

Before proceeding it may be useful to clarify our use of the terms *masculinities* and *femininities*. The term *masculinities* is used to avoid both the

From the *Australian Journal of Language and Literacy*, 21(2), June 1998. Reprinted with permission of the authors and the Australian Literacy Educators' Association.

tendency to treat abstract concepts as if they have a concrete reality and the suggestion that there is some single, common essence to being male (despite the strategic importance of essentialism on occasions). For instance, Segal (1990) explores a range of competing masculinities from "tough guys" and "martial men," from homosexuals through to black masculinity, and considers aspects of male domination and violence. Similarly, Connell (1989) also describes a range of masculinities ranging from "cool guys," "swots" and "wimps." As with masculinity, femininity is not a monolithic discourse but there are many feminisms (Luke & Gore, 1992).

Our interests in studying masculinity and education

Why should men, and ourselves in particular, be interested in the socially critical study of men and masculinities? Firstly, and most consciously, our interest in issues of masculinity arises from our concerns about social injustice in education. By and large, gender is a taken-for-granted feature of educational life. Of course, there are many occasions when this habitual disregard is interrupted and we are challenged to rethink the gendered nature of institutionalised education. For instance, there are those times when some female teachers express concern about being powerless and being denied significant authority in school decision making. Or when a male teacher complains about the school curriculum for its culturally imperialist representation of humanity, constructed from an exclusively white, masculine perspective, rendering the interests of ethnic minority women invisible at the same time as stereotyping them.

As well as this explicit focus on studying masculinities, we must admit that other motives for our interest in this of study are complex, contradictory and overlapping. No doubt we need to think much more, and more critically, about our motivations for addressing gender issues in education and the possible consequences these may have. For the time being we acknowledge those motivations (no doubt there are others of which we are not presently conscious) which arise from our recognition that:

- it is necessary for men to turn our attention to those aspects of gender not widely problematised at present, namely men and masculinities;

- it is our reaction against liberal and radical feminisms, and tendencies towards separatism and reductionism;

- it is because we identify with social and cultural feminist women, in part as a consequence of our own life experiences, and in part because their scholarship gives a basis for questioning the rigid, dominant model of masculinity;
- the arguments and theories of these feminists are just, and as a consequence we acknowledge our complicity in sexual oppression and out of this we have developed a concern for the cultural politics of gender difference and the ethics of sexual injustices;
- there is a need to explore the contradictions between school-based literacy participation and dominant forms of masculinity.

In summary, whatever our implicit or explicit motives for this area of interest, we are much less interested in celebrating or defending patriarchy or dominant forms of masculinity than we are in contributing to these efforts to make dominant masculinities problematic. In the course of normal events, a patriarchal education system does not call upon men to make their gender problematic, as it does for women.

The social formation of masculinities

There is no single "traditional" or "dominant" masculinity, but rather an array of differently accented masculinities ranging from hegemonic to subordinate through complicitous to marginal (Connell, 1995). Men's sense of masculine identity is subject to change due to the interplay of history and experience. For example, encounters with feminism may be awkward or even painful, especially for those whose masculinity is mediated by other identities, such as being gay or of a racial/ethnic minority background. For some men gender may not be the most important element in their identity; there is a need to consider the intersection of gender with other social factors such as class and ethnic/racial identities.

There is not merely a diversity of masculinities, but masculinities are linked to each other. There is a hierarchical relationship, based on power, between men and women, as well as between some men and other men, for instance between authoritarian white males and half-caste Eurasian males (mulattos).

The construction of dominant forms of masculinity relates to the control and domination of women and to other forms of masculinity. Patriarchy is both "about the domination of men over women and some men over some other men and about the relationships between these two sets of dominations" (Morgan, 1992, p. 202). For example, bullying and fighting in the school playground between non-Aboriginal and Aboriginal boys is not simply a rehearsal for the exercise of power over women but also the exercise of power by some men over certain types of men. What it feels like to be a man can only be adequately answered in the context of gendered encounters, especially encounters where sexual or gender differences are accented, including difference in masculinity. Masculinity is something which emerges out of and is constituted through gendered encounters, and through these interactions one gains a certain masculinity. We adopt a *relational approach* of masculinities whereby these are seen as being evoked, created or sustained through day-to-day interactions. Of course, individuals do not have complete freedom as to which version of masculinity they express or suppress in particular encounters. Any society has a range of historically shaped masculinities which are hierarchically arranged, but not in a fixed fashion. Masculinities are determined by the demands of the particular situation and by the array of masculinities that may be available and privileged (such as in children's picture books). Gender is negotiated in a range of situations, and so, as Morgan (1992) argues, we need to think of *doing masculinities* rather than being masculine.

Male responses to feminisms

There have been various responses by men to the differing schools of feminist theory and practice. Perhaps most men have not been significantly affected by feminism at all, their position of power and privilege allowing them to be indifferent to those they have subordinated. Of course, there are those who have been influenced by one form of feminism or another, although not all in the same way. No doubt a number of white male patriarchs have opportunistically allied themselves to feminism so as to exploit feminist concerns in order to advance their own self-interests. All the same, some men have begun to question the position of men in society and the dominant constructions of masculinity especially as represented in educational contexts.

For the moment it might be useful to think of men who have responded to feminisms, in one way or another, as being either anti-feminist men, pro-male men or pro-feminist men. It is important, though, to be cautious about using these categories: while they provide a useful way of classifying men's responses to the various feminisms, masculinity is much more complex and ambiguous than such a typology suggests.

Another focus for critical literacy

Just as there are various approaches to critical literacy (see Said, 1993; Fairclough, 1992), there are also various approaches to the critical study of men and masculinities, only some of which are likely to provide useful insights into what it feels like to be a man. For example, it is possible to examine cases where men and masculinity explicitly come to the fore in single sex schools and sport. The following section discusses one specific pedagogical strategy for making masculinities the focus of critical literacy. It is not an innocent strategy and so requires a critical examination of the assumptions that lie behind this teaching practice. Lankshear (1994, p. 9ff.) suggests that critical literacy could involve all or any of the following aspects:

a. knowing literacy (or various literacies) critically, that is, having a critical perspective on *literacy/literacies* generally;

b. having a critical/evaluative perspective on particular *texts*;

c. having a critical perspective on—i.e., being able to make "critical readings" of—wider *social practices, arrangements, relations, allocations, procedures, etc.* which are mediated and made possible by, and partially sustained through, the reading of texts.

Pallotta-Chiarolli (1994, p. 44) argues that "the English classroom can become a terrain of intervention and resistance in analysing and dismantling stereotypes and assumptions about masculinities." One possible strategy is to re-examine commonly used school texts to reveal the "taken for granted" stories they have to tell about men and masculinities.

Gilbert (1988) makes the point that, despite prevailing perspectives to the contrary, reading is a *political* act. According to Freebody (1992), students should be encouraged to take on the role of *text-analyst* and encouraged to develop alternative readings through looking further into the ideologies of the text to determine: Who is in power? What are the socio-cultural factors associated with the composition of the text? What is being portrayed as natural? What emotions are being attached to the participants? Who or what is left out of the text? Do all participants play an active role? From whose perspective is this being written? It is in this context that Gilbert (1988, p. 15) argues that approaches

> to reading which have assumed a personal response from a reader to a text—
> without considering the cultural construction of such a response and such a
> reading practice—have more recently been challenged by critical appraisals of

the nature of reading and writing practices, and of the nature of literacy and literary production. Such challenges make it easier to understand some of the complexities of "reading like a man" or "reading like a woman...."

Our proposal here is based on Morgan's (1992) work (and follows Freebody's [1992] explanation of text-analyst) which suggests that we focus on teaching the reading skills associated with critical literacy such as identifying gaps and silences in the text. We need to explicitly teach students to re-read and re-write school texts from multiple perspectives, most importantly from the perspective of *the self-critical, pro-feminist man*. Before expanding on and providing an illustrative example of this strategy, it is necessary to define what is meant by the *self-critical, pro-feminist man* and to define *re-reading* in terms of school-based literacy competencies.

The pro-feminist man

There is no single *pro-feminist* position, especially given that there is a series of feminisms ranging from literal, social and cultural through to radical feminism. Some pro-feminist men have responded by challenging or rejecting prescribed masculine roles within the family. Others have shown unease about dominant models of masculinity and have moved away from a defence of patriarchy. These changes have been reinforced by the actual relationships these men have with particular women. There are men who recognise that the activities they engage in as school managers and/or teachers are gendered ones. Recognising their gendered character, they no longer take such activities for granted, but seek to expose the inequitable relationships between female and male educators.

The self-critical, pro-feminist man

The existence of pro-feminist males may suggest that changes are occurring in masculinities, or it may reflect the on-going presence of a mode of masculinity that has always been present in society, albeit a marginalised form of masculinity. Here we would like to refer to Morgan's (1992) discussion of the rise of one type of pro-feminist man, that of the *self-critical man*. This man is highly literate, having been inspired by research in women's studies and the need for a positive response to feminism. Reading and engaging with feminist research, scholarship and critiques have been the *self-critical man's* major stimulant for the study of men and masculinities. In one sense this topic—the explicit study of men and masculinities as such—did not exist until feminists provided the assumptions and recognition of the importance of gender divisions in social (power) relations, and brought to the fore the imbalances in thought and actions between men and women in order to question, criticise and change. The experiences and writing of gay, Eurasian and black men have explored relations between men and highlighted the need to recognise a multiplicity of masculinities.

Re-reading

Reading may be understood as a social (or public) activity. It is social in that the act of reading, whether private or not, is an act embedded in a wider nexus of social relations, just as the production of a text is also a form of social production. To read a book, and especially to read a school book, is to enter into relationships which are not simply with the text itself but, intertextually, with a host of other readers and texts. In schools this is a formalised pedagogic practice. Typically, students are required to read a chapter or passage (from a text also being read by their peers) and then participate in a discussion on that reading with other students and their teacher. Similarly, in writing essays, students may be encouraged to read what others have had to say about the particular text in question. The selection of a school text, and the practices for reading it, are of course social processes; they are highly dependent on people who have a stake in the production and perpetuation of both the texts' and pedagogies' reputation in schools. Thus, school reading is never a purely innocent activity.

Even when reading a text for the first time, we come to it with certain expectations which are generated through interpersonal interactions or various prior assumptions; in part, these expectations are created by previous readings and how we have been taught to read. Students will have certain expectations of a text because of its location in a particular Key Learning Area, through comments made by peers in classes, and through previous teacher-led discussions of other texts. Re-reading is a critical literacy strategy which means that students and teacher

> return to a text with the sounds of other texts echoing in our minds and with the memories of previous texts and discussions interacting with the present rereading.... [Rereading] also has some feature of novelty about it...to see this text in a slightly different light.... [Thus] every reading is both a first reading and a rereading. (Morgan, 1992, p. 50).

In part, English teaching is about helping students to learn to reread texts in socially critical ways. They need to be taught how to read between the lines, to seek out themes which may not be explicitly stated, to read for absences as well as presences, to decode the text in order to discover hidden or suppressed meanings. The processes of re-reading different genres is not necessarily the same: critical literacy is a complex social activity. Gender is part of the often "taken for granted" stories that school texts have to tell (we do not think they are "hidden" as much as taken for granted). The question is, "How can we learn to read books written by males about men as if they are about making problematic issues of masculinity?"

Re-reading means learning to be active in reading, not passive, learning to read texts in new ways and from new perspectives; it means developing the skills of critical literacy. In recent years feminist scholars have shown us ways to examine texts for their problematic construction of women and girls and draw attention to omissions (Gilbert, 1988). The point of such pedagogies is not just to highlight the injustices of a *blind spot* or invisibility in the curriculum, but to demonstrate that including *women* in the frame of reference for reading a text affects such reading by providing new knowledge and new insights.

As with issues of class, it is not that men and male experiences are totally absent from texts. There is, however, a lack of educated readers (both men and women) who can read these texts in ways that critically foreground issues of masculinity, or at least institutional legitimisation and support for doing so. While an overabundance of material exists about certain types of men, issues of masculinity are typically not deliberately, explicitly or critically addressed. Thus, we are faced with the problem of selecting from the sheer volume of material available. Any text being used for educational purposes requires a multiplicity of re-readings, exploring how it speaks to different people at different times in different ways. Thus, a particular school text book might be read as a text about men, being read in particular for the attitudes it reveals different types of men as having with regard to:

- women
- sexuality
- marriage
- the development of certain kinds of masculinities
- the division between home and paid work
- the divisions between private and public
- the spheres of women's and men's lives, and

- the relation between being a responsible person and being responsible for others (as opposed to just helping).

The following are examples of questions which might guide the critical re-reading of a school text, questions which have been framed from a feminist perspective to make problematic men and masculinities.

- In what ways can school texts be used to provide a study of masculinity?
- How far can a school text which happens to be about men also be read as a text about masculinity, male domination/subordination, and the struggle by certain types of men to gain and maintain power over women and other men?
- Can school texts provide studies of (what Morgan [1992] terms) men's *homo-sociability* (i.e., the maintenance of certain kinds of relationships between men and women, and between certain types of men, such as the preference of some men for each others' company)?
- Which of these relationships are located in public or semi-public sites?
- What do school texts reveal about the particular sets of exchanges and interdependencies that grow up between different types of men (e.g., in-group tenderness, mutual concern)?
- Do school texts show us both the centrifugal and centripetal sources of variations within masculine culture (such as self-interested ambition, aggressiveness or bullying and manipulation or exploitation which threaten values of respect, decency and mutual obligations)?
- How much can school texts tell us about masculinities in all their complexities and diversities?
- Are women, as represented in school texts, seen only through the eyes of men or are they hidden altogether?

School texts are not simply a source of information, but rather a text is something that mediates relationships between readers and other people, and as such the process of reading deserves as much attention as the actual words of the text.

Students of all ages need to be encouraged to *re-write* meanings of texts and to learn from the efforts of others to do so. In working with groups of secondary students studying Mary Durack's poem, *Red Jack*, Kenworthy (1994, p. 36) "wanted to help the students to understand better the relationship between text and aspects of context like audience, purpose and background." Accordingly, he

> asked them to write a letter which would subvert the men's view of Red Jack; a letter which would subvert the masculine construct of Red Jack as "strange"; a letter which would allow her the internal life which had been denied her in the poem; a letter which would provide her with a past and a future, a letter which would show her as fully human.
> (Kenworthy, 1994, p. 36)

Problematic aspects of developing re-readers and re-writers

It is important to note here that these classroom practices are not without problems. Pallotta-Chiarolli (1994, p. 45) reports that "resistance [to these types of strategies] from students, parents and other staff may be forthcoming." She also makes a point about "the position of the English teacher" and his/her level of "subjectivity or objectivity" (Pallotta-Chiarolli, 1994, p. 45). Teachers need to be clear about their own ideologies and values in relation to gender and power if they are to justly work as a facilitator of critical literacy with students in the class. All students need to be given the opportunity to express their views in a supportive environment while still being clear about how their views can impinge on other students.

Alloway and Gilbert (1997, p. 55) argue that the critical literacy strategies that teachers want to implement in order to help boys look at the ways in which masculinities are constructed in school texts, and then re-read these texts, may be "incompatible with their understandings of appropriate masculine identity." The strategy of re-reading texts asks students to be reflective and reflexive in their practices, whereas

> hegemonic masculinity prefers to concentrate on things outside of self, rather than on the self. Some groups of boys may find the pressure to become insiders to the literacy experience particularly threatening to the masculinity. (Alloway & Gilbert, 1997, p. 56)

Kenworthy (1994, p. 34) relates a classroom situation where, despite the fact that much work had gone into developing *resistant reading* strategies with a group of boys, the boys' attitude seemed to be "...we want to resist your resistant readings." They resisted the idea that social and discursive practices construct forms of masculinity whether to promote them, intensify them or subvert them. Kenworthy argues that this particular group of boys set out to subvert his lesson. When asked to complete a

rewriting task (as explained above) the boys refused "...to write against the social roles [and practices] that they have spent most of their lives learning,
and in which, at this age, they have a very strong investment" (Hogan,
cited in Kenworthy, 1994, p. 39). He adds: "by adopting a feminine reader/
writer positioning they ran the risk of being constructed by their peers
through discourse as feminine" (p. 39).

Problems of studying men and masculinities

Given that hegemonic males see the world largely as being of and
for men, and humanity represented by men of certain sexual orientations
and racial and class backgrounds, the study of men and masculinity presents many problems. Attempts by men to study themselves must always
be suspect since it is their (our) power that feminism has challenged.

The study of men cannot be separated from issues of sexual and gender politics; men do benefit from the subordination of women. We admit
that for us the study of men has a key credibility problem: men are not
widely oppressed (as men, although in terms of class and race/ethnicity
some certainly are), nor do they seem to have common grievances to air (as
men). In other words, men need to be careful that through their (our) self-
critique there is not a tendency for the outcome to be the legitimising of
existing power relationships and in fact serve to further entrench existing
power relationships between men and women, and men and men, and to
perpetuate a narrow view of what it means to be masculine. Following
Davies (1997, p. 25) we see re-reading and re-writing as opening up

> the possibility of students and teachers becoming reflexively aware of the way
> in which speaking-as-usual constructs themselves and others. And so it opens
> up the possibility of thinking/writing/speaking in quite different ways, ways
> that enable boys to position themselves in multiple subjectivities which they
> can recognise and claim as their own despite regimes of truth that dictate other-
> wise.

Conclusion

Without feminist thought and practice the problems addressed in this
article are unlikely to have been raised. Feminism provides a comprehensive
challenge to all aspects of patriarchal society and the prevailing gender order. Feminist critiques also encourage some men to problematise issues of
men and masculinities, especially those self-critical, pro-feminist men. In re-

sponse to feminist critiques there are various strategies that can be adopted for the socially critical study of men and masculinities. One possible strategy for use in the English classroom builds upon the tradition of critical literacy, namely teaching students to re-read and re-write texts that are about men and masculinities from the perspective of the *self-critical, profeminist man*. The focus of this teaching strategy is not the biological differences between men and women, but how and why these differences are accented and given social, cultural and economic significance. Hegemonic forms of masculinity are not disregarded but rather the purpose is to deconstruct them. Likewise, the aim of this strategy is to develop English classrooms that highlight and celebrate a wide range of masculinities, in particular *literate masculinities*.

While the study of men and masculinity is fraught with various difficulties, it may not be an impossibility. As males we need to explore our own curriculum practices as well as efforts to change the educational institutions in which we work. There is no reason why some men, if not all, might not come to understand their role in a patriarchal society and seek ways of transforming that system. The underlying point of this article is that our distinctive contribution as men to the struggle against sexism, patriarchy and literacy problems might be based on critiques of men's practices and oppressive models of masculinities, and may well start with taken-for-granted school texts, such as children's picture books.

REFERENCES

Alloway, N., & Gilbert, P. (1997). Boys and literacy: Lessons from Australia. *Gender and Education, 9*(1), 49–58.

Cameron, P. (1997). Animal house. *The Australian Magazine*, February 1/2, pp. 9–13.

Cameron, P. (1997). *Finishing school for blokes.* Sydney: Allen & Unwin.

Connell, R. (1989). Cool guys, swots and wimps: The interplay of masculinity and education. *Oxford Review of Education, 15*(3), 291–303.

Davies, B. (1997). Constructing and deconstructing masculinities through critical literacy. *Gender and Education, 9*(1), 9–30.

Fairclough, N. (1992). *Critical language awareness.* London: Longman.

Freebody, P. (1992). A socio-cultural approach: Resourcing four roles as a literacy learner. In A. Watson and A. Badenhop (Eds.), *Prevention of reading failure.* Sydney: Ashton Scholastic.

Gilbert, P. (1988). Stoning the romance: Girls as resistant readers and writers. *Curriculum Perspectives, 8*(2), 13–8.

Griffin, P. (1989). Homophobia in physical education. *Canadian Journal of Health and Physical Education, 55*(2), 27–31.

Griffin, P., & Genasci, J. (1990). Addressing homophobia in physical education: Suggestions for teachers and researchers. In D. Sabo & M. Messner (Eds.), *Sport, men and the gender order: Critical feminist perspectives.* Champaign, IL: Human Kenetics.

Harding S. (1986). *The science question in feminism.* Ithaca, NY: Cornell University Press.

Kenworthy, C. (1994). We want to resist your resistant readings: Masculinity and discourse in the English classroom. *Opinion, 24*(4), 33–43.

Lankshear, C. (1994). *Critical literacy.* Occasional paper. Belconnen, ACT: Australian Curriculum Studies Association.

Lingard, B., Henry, M., & Taylor, S. (1987). A girl in a militant pose: A chronology of struggle in girls' education in Queensland. *British Journal of Sociology of Education, 8*(2), 135–52.

Luke, C., & Gore, J. (Eds.). (1992). *Feminisms and critical pedagogy.* New York: Routledge.

McHoul, A. (1984). Writing, sexism and schooling: A discourse-analytic investigation of some recent documents on sexism and education in Queensland. *Discourse, 4*(2), 1–17.

Morgan, D. (1992). *Discovering men.* London: Routledge.

Pallotta-Chiarolli, M. (1994). Butch minds the baby: Boys minding masculinity in the English classroom. *Opinion, 24*(4), 44–50.

Said, E. (1993). *Culture and imperialism.* London: Chatto and Windus.

Segal, L. (1990). *Slow motion: Changing masculinities, changing men.* London: Virago Press.

Critical Literacy and Pop Music Magazines

Lorraine Wilson

In 1997 I interviewed upper school children in two Melbourne primary schools about their reading habits. I learnt that pop music magazines are "devoured" by children of this age group. In fact the text which scored highest as the favourite for out of school hours was "Smash Hits," closely followed by "TV Hits."

In this article I focus on some critical literacy work done as part of an integrated unit of work called "MUSIC," with teachers Laureen Thompson and Jenni Smith and their Grade 3/4/5 students. Our teaching focus was reader as text analyst, as per the four resources model of Freebody and Luke. Of course concurrent with being text analysts, the children were code breakers, text participants and text users.

In fact, the children made many uses of these popular everyday texts. I learnt that they purchased them: to learn the words of the current hit songs; to get the free posters included; to decorate their bedroom walls; to learn about their favourite stars and current heart throbs; and to better participate with their peer culture.

The teaching focus in this unit was the choices writers face as they write, and the connection between the choices made and the possible manipulation of meanings for the reader.

Lessons 1 & 2

In each of these lessons the children were given copies of interviews published in "Smash Hits." One was with the group Hanson and the other with Cleopatra. The children were required to:

• read the interview

From *Practically Primary*, 4(2), June 1999. Reprinted with permission of the author and the Australian Literacy Educators' Association.

• write what they learnt about the group from reading the article
• write what the article did not tell them about the performers' lives.

Generally the children found it difficult to write about the aspects of the performers' lives not mentioned in the articles. Some did note that there was no mention of schooling, friends or pets.

However, although these interviews were with pop stars, none of the children wondered why there was no information about practice or rehearsals or how the stars learnt music. None of the children identified this information gap.

Lesson 3

In this lesson the children were given only the question (not the answers) asked in an interview with "Bachelor Girl" and published in "Smash Hits." The article was called "ROCK STAR OR PUSSYCAT?...to find out if they have what it takes to cut it in the biz!"

The answers were removed to help the children focus on the writer's part in shaping the interview.

ROCK STAR OR PUSSYCAT?
1. When was the last time you stayed up all night?
2. When was the last time you got into a brawl?
3. When was the last time you got kicked out of a club?
4. Have you ever travelled in a limousine?
5. Has anyone famous ever asked you for an autograph?
6. Do you have a tattoo?
7. Would you get your tongue pierced?
8. Have you ever smashed up an instrument on stage?
9. When was the last time you stage dived?

The children were asked to write why the interviewer asked these questions and not other questions.

Only a small number of the children had some insight into why these questions might have been asked:

Mitchell: Because they want to get inside them and rip out their inside feelings.

Harrison: These Qs are a bit unfair and personal for the person who is doing the As. The journalist is asking these Qs to find out from the As if the person who is doing the As is weak or the opposite.

Eugene: I think the reporter is asking stupid questions to see how they react. I think he is trying to see how they handle it.

Other children thought the journalist asked these questions just to be different:

Bridget: I think they ask these questions because they're different. Usually they ask questions like what your favourite hobbies are, and so people don't get bored.

Tom: To ask questions that people would not ask.

Lesson 4

Because many of the children were finding it hard to stand back from the text and to wonder why particular questions were being asked, two questionnaires about the students' lives were designed for them to an-

---

QUESTIONNAIRE 1

1. What is your Grandma like?
2. What is the kindest thing you have ever done?
3. Which is your favourite icecream flavour?
4. How do you help your Mum and Dad at home?
5. What do you read in bed?
6. What do you want to be when you grow up?

QUESTIONNAIRE 2

1. When did you last have a fight?
2. What's the worst thing you have ever done?
3. Have you ever shoplifted?
4. When are you mean to your brothers and sisters?
5. When you are really angry what do you do?
6. How loud do you like to play your music?
7. What do you want to be when you grow up?

swer. The purpose here was to show how particular questions can shape a particular image.

Asking children to answer such questions certainly aroused them:

Bridget: But it is none of your business. I think some of these questions are a bit privet and personnell like what is the worst thing you have ever done or have you ever shoplifted. Sorry I don't think this should be your business but I filled it out anyway.

When all children had completed the questionnaire, I read some of the responses to the whole group, not mentioning the authors' names. I read the responses to Questionnaire 1 from one child and asked: "What sort of person is this?"

I then read the responses to Questionnaire 2 from the same child without letting on to the children it was the same child, and asked the same question, "What sort of person is this?"

I then revealed, "But this is the same child! How come we get such different pictures of this one child?"

The children began at last to connect the interview questions with the image created! They then wrote some notes about how the two different interviews made them look.

Harrison: Questionnaire 1. This page can make a person look like he's made of gold. It does this by focusing on all the good things. Questionnaire 2. This page can destroy someone. It does this by focusing on all the bad things.

Andrew: Questionnaire 1. This side I sound goody goody really nice because these are goody goody questions. They make me sound like I don't have a bad side to me. Questionnaire 2. This side makes me sound really bad like I just had a fight two hours ago and I punch people when I'm angry.

Wing Hing,
Grade 5:   Questionnaire 1. It sounds like they're doing nothing, just getting friendly, the questions. It's like trying to take away the shyness and hoping you'll cooperate with them. They're trying to get people to think this person is warm and friendly and great, buy their stuff! The questions are trying to make you honest so when they want to pursue

your feelings, you voice them out. Questionnaire 2. This is like trying to get you to be a party animal, like a rock star. They make you look wild.

Brad,
Grade 4: Questionnaire 1. I think these questions made me look like the nicest person on the planet. Questionnaire 2. These questions made me look like a person you wouldn't like to meet in a dark alley.

At last the children were beginning to see the writer as other than neutral: that the writer in these magazines was making choices about the questions posed, and importantly, how different questions created different pictures of the same subject.

Following lessons

In following lessons the children wrote questions they wished to ask their favourite groups. As well, in small groups, the children identified print features of these magazines (for example, free gifts, short articles, lots of colour, many photographs) and tried to give reasons for the use of these design features. Then as a class they went on to produce their own pop music magazine: "SIXTEEN'S SUPER COOL MUSIC MAG."

Literacy and the New Technologies in School Education: Meeting the L(IT)eracy Challenge?

Cal Durrant and Bill Green

Introduction

Literacy *is* changing. Once it was entirely shaped by the technologies of the printing and publishing industries and their associated cultures. Now, however, in an age of burgeoning new media of communication, information, and representation, there are more and different technologies available. These are increasingly deployed in working and playing with texts, in the practice of new and different literacies. Indeed, we are now able to recognise and acknowledge that, for schooling and education, print is simply one of a range of available technocultural resources. Accordingly, account needs to be taken of a profound media shift in literacy, schooling and society—a broad-based shift from print to digital electronics as the organising context for literature-textual practice and for learning and teaching. Although this does not mean the eclipse of print technologies and cultures, it does mean that we need to employ a rather different, more flexible and comprehensive view of literacy than teachers are used to in both their work and their lives. Print takes a new place within a reconceptualised understanding of literacy, schooling and technological practice, one which is likely to be beneficial in moving us and our children into a new millennium.

In this article, we seek to provide some guidance for teachers in thinking through and towards this "sea-change" in literacy and education, particularly as it relates to and is likely to impact on schooling in New South Wales, and in Australia more generally. This is a topic of considerable turmoil and flux at this time, and it would be foolish to try to make firm predictions for the future, or even for the day after tomorrow.

From the *Australian Journal of Language and Literacy*, 23(2), June 2000. Reprinted with permission of the authors and the Australian Literacy Educators' Association.

However it is possible to present and examine some principles and practices and provide an introduction to what is now emerging as a significant knowledge-base in this area. We believe that such an examination is likely to be helpful in teachers' classroom planning and professional development. We shall begin with an overview of the context, and also of some of the existing terms of debate and outcomes of research. Following that, we will outline a model or framework for school practice and educational policy, consistent with and informed by both current policy initiatives in New South Wales and elsewhere, and also current scholarly and professional work towards a practical theory of literacy, IT and schooling.[1]

Changing contexts and new economies

It is estimated that there are over 43 million hosts connected to the Internet worldwide, and somewhere between 40 and 80 million adults in the United States alone have access to around 320 million unique pages of content on arguably one of the most important communication innovations in history (Hoffman & Novak 1999).

As a nation, Australia is also adopting technology-driven environments with increasing enthusiasm, as computer chips become ever more versatile and pervasive. The Australian Bureau of Statistics reports that in 1999, almost 23% of Australian households were connected to the Internet. Significantly, of these 1.6 million households, almost 71% were located in capital cities, and the heaviest users are the young: more than 74% of 18–24 year olds accessed the Internet in the 12 months to August 1999 and some 52% of 25–39 year olds. For those aged between 40 and 54 years, however, the figure drops to 39% and a mere 13% for persons 55 years and over (Australian Bureau of Statistics, 1999).

Over the next decade, Web usage is expected to increase dramatically. The 1999 CommerceNet/Nielsen Internet Demographic Survey (CommerceNet, 1999) suggest that over 90 million Americans are regular users, and this is expected to increase to over 150 million over the next couple of years. Electronic commerce is also predicted to explode. Anderson Consulting predicts that an estimated 200,000 American households are currently purchasing their food and household goods on-line (compare this with the 652,000 Australians who are ordering goods and

---

[1.] This paper was originally prepared as a Discussion Paper for the NSW Department of Education and Training—hence some of its references and sources.

services on-line), but by 2007, that number is expected to hit 20 million (Dirkson, 1998). So where does all this new technology fit in with our hard-won and now well-established views about literacy?

Recent moves in international education policies confirm that governments the world over are becoming more and more committed to a technology-saturated future. In 1998, the United Kingdom spent £220 million (funded by the National Lottery) on technology in education. In Singapore around $2 billion was set aside to be spent over five years along similar lines. The U.S. government also approved in 1998 a five-year, $2 billion program called the Technology Challenge Literacy Fund; its primary purposes being to encourage "computer literacy" and to connect schools to the Internet by the year 2000 (Techsetter, 1998).

Here in Australia, which is second only to the United States in its per-household use of personal computers, state governments are equally intent on ensuring that Australian students of the twenty-first century are given every opportunity of participating in and benefiting from this bright new world that will demand technologically skilled workforces if countries and nations are both to keep pace with change and position themselves favourably in an increasingly global economy.

In 1998, the Victorian government committed $51.4 m for access to computers, the Internet, on-line curriculum materials, and technology training for teachers (*Education Review* 1998, April, p. 9). Similarly, over four years the Western Australian government pledged $100 m to similar projects (*Inform* 1998, June, p. 17). Tasmanian students living outside metropolitan areas are soon to be supplied with access to on-line training and education, while the Northern Territory is set to install PCs in all schools and throughout their Department. In NSW, $184 m is being spent over four years on computer and information technology in schools, including a number of new modes of delivery for development and training of teachers, like CD-ROM, Web-based training, email support and video conferencing.

It is rather unusual to hear of such large sums of money being thrown at education, particularly for such specific goals, but technology seems to have been taken on board the education "band-wagon." Time will tell if the hype has substance; but in the meantime, our notions of literacy are undergoing dramatic changes as we struggle to keep up with the digital revolution.

Technology: More than just an "add-on"?

Traditionally, technology has always been treated as something of an "add-on" when considered in relation to literacy. As Bruce has observed: "We don't notice the technologies of literacy because we treat our literacy technologies as natural and inevitable" (Bruce, 1998, p. 47). If you stop and think about it, it is difficult to imagine using anything other than pen-and-paper or a word-processor in the act of writing; it's just what we *do*—though it is worth remembering that others before us found the use of sharpened stones, blackened sticks, coals, chalk, quills or fountain pens equally natural and unremarkable.

The fact that we rarely stop to think about the technologies we use in relation to literacy practices probably suggests that they are very deeply embedded in our daily routines. Indeed, some commentators have suggested that initial teacher resistance to new technologies is often a result of the fact that we, as teachers, are the products of those very technologies we once thought we simply used (Hoskin, 1993, p. 27). Historically, it is clear that each new advance in technology has pushed back the boundaries of what was formerly possible. But as can be seen in Table 1 below, with every new advance has come a corresponding change in our conception of literacy and its role in society.

What strikes us as being of particular interest about the various literacy debates in recent times is that proponents of some points of view—specifically those who argue from an exclusively print-dominant standpoint—appear to have established fixed points for their own litera-

---

TABLE 1
Literacy transformations

---

primitive symbol systems
　　↳complex oral language
　　　　↳early writing
　　　　　　↳manuscript literacy
　　　　　　　　↳print literacy
　　　　　　　　　　↳video literacy
　　　　　　　　　　　　↳digital/multimedia/hypertext literacy
　　　　　　　　　　　　↳virtual reality

(Bruce, 1998, p. 47)

cy stances, in defiance of the fact that the creation of new technologies continues to change society's concept of literacy, *just as it has always done.*

This is not to suggest that print-literacy is old-fashioned, "dead-in-the-water," or unworthy of our most exacting attention. It simply means that we are moving beyond the constraints of literacy practices that are purely print-based. As educators, we should both recognise this and be positioning ourselves to take advantage of what is and can become possible in terms of such practices with each technological advance. Clearly, we are not saying here that teachers, schools or Departments of Education should enthusiastically and perhaps ingenuously veer into every newly enticing detour on the information superhighway. Rather, what we are suggesting is that nothing should be necessarily eliminated from our lists of items of potential usefulness just because it does not fit our current notions of literacy.

Literacy policies and new proposals

Indeed, the 1997 position paper on the teaching of literacy in New South Wales, *Focus on Literacy,* has clearly recognized the need for such forward thinking. In adopting the concept of literacy proposed by the writers of the companion volume to *Australia's Language* (1991), in which literacy is defined as being "the ability to read and use written information and to write appropriately, in a range of contexts," it also drew attention to the fact that:

> Since 1991, the very nature of what constitutes literacy has been expanded by the emerging multimedia and information technologies, the appearance of the Internet and further developments in computing and word processing. (NSW DSE, 1997, p. 8)

As with everything else in our world, our notions about what it is to be "literate" are ever in a state of flux. While it is necessary to have explicit and systematic strategies that address the current needs of literacy teachers, it is equally imperative that we are able to clearly identify, target and adopt new literacy practices and possibilities as they arise.

What is often forgotten in debates about the new technologies and their impact on literacy is that they *are* indeed, by definition, *new.* While it is true that computers and their high-technology relatives have been used in schools at least since the early 1980s, it is equally true that, until very recently, for many teachers they were a force to be either resisted or disdainfully ignored (Bigum, 1993, p. 81). It is interesting that as recently as 1990 there could have been a book published in Australia under the futuristic title *Literacy for a Changing World*, edited by one of the most respected literacy educators in the country, that all but ignored technology and its role in the literacy debate (Christie, 1990). While it did rate a brief mention in the opening chapter, it was only as an apologetic aside:

> While the computer, the word processor and even the fax machine certainly have had an impact in educational settings...they are probably still less a feature of daily life there than they are in other parts of our society, and consequently many teachers know less about them than they might.
> (Christie, 1990, p. 22)[2]

Such a cursory reference to the relationship between technology and literacy is even more curious when we take into consideration the 1991 Christie Report, which included the following recommendation on pre-service teacher preparation:

> That all students should be required to learn to use computers in their course work, with the aim of attaining a basic technological proficiency in at least the following: word processing, principles of electronic text design and publication; using printers, modems and other peripheral devices; designing hypermedia programs; and exchanging electronic data on a network. (Christie et al., 1991, p. 223)

Such apparent contradictions are not unusual for the time period (cf. Green and Bigum, 1996). The investigators on the Children's Literacy National Project, *Digital Rhetorics*, examined the national policy climate in relation to literacy and technology in state syllabus and Commonwealth policy documents, identifying a very mixed state in the literature up until the early to mid 1990s. While various state computer/technology policies existed in the eighties, the general scene has until very recently been a largely confused one marked by:

> many different groups doing things, apparently unaware, perhaps simply not interested, in the activities and pursuits of other groups, despite the possibility that they may share similar agendas.... The result has been the creation of related but essentially discrete IT policies, Literacy policies and Education and other policies. (Lankshear et al., 1997, p. 149 [Vol.1])

---

[2] Note, in contrast, a more recently edited volume (eds. Christie & Misson, 1998), which is much more explicit and focused in its attention to IT with regard to literacy and schooling.

Australia as an Information Society (1991), under the direction of Barry Jones, was perhaps the first national document to usher in a somewhat belated consideration of the so-called information society and its implications for the nation (Lankshear et al., 1997, p. 94 [Vol. 1]). As for clear and specific links being established between literacy and technology, little eventuated until the publication of *Australian Literacies* (Lo Bianco & Freebody 1997), which does take into account the uses and significance of the new technologies in literacy education. On the school education front more broadly, however, towards the middle of the 1990s there was a growing insistence on the use of the new technologies, so much so that comments and attitudes such as those expressed by leading Australian educators Fazal Rizvi and Bob Lingard, in the foreword to a recent book on computers and literacy (Snyder, 1997), appear now to be a reflection of the norm rather than the exception:

> The essays in this collection are based on a conviction that the new information technologies have the capacity to fundamentally transform all of our cultural practices, including those associated with schooling.... Students are not going to wait for their teachers to catch up with the new textual practices that they already prefer. Teachers will have to come to terms with this new computer-mediated communication world. They will have to devise new ways of thinking about literacy in which both the page and the screen are brought together. (Rizvi & Lingard, 1997, p. xii)

It seems to us that statements like this represent something of a dramatic turnaround in attitude. In New South Wales, such imperatives were boosted by the State Labor Government's Computers in Schools Policy [CISP] (ALP, 1995) and the establishment of the Department's TILT (Technology in Learning and Teaching) program, that enabled a wide spectrum of classroom teachers across the State to both gain a working knowledge of and become enthusiastic about the use of technology in their teaching. The latter's success can be partly measured by the degree of interstate and international interest in the monitoring of its development and implementation.

Of course, we know from past experience that new technologies don't simply replace established systems of communication; rather they produce hybrid forms. But what is perhaps different about the second-wave information technologies is the rapidity of such changes.

> The spread of alphabetic literacy took thousands of years and continues to this day. The development of the practices and artefacts of the printing press spread

unevenly across Europe over a 300-year period. In less than 40 years, television has become a principal global technology of human communication, commerce, political life, and public education. In two decades, the computer has gone from exclusive, specialised business and research tool to common household appliance. (Luke & Elkins, 1998, p. 6)

Just how do we go about shifting our strategies for teaching more or less print-bound literacy to helping our students meet the fresh demands and challenges of literacies that spring from living in such technologised and seamless "new times"?

Before we leave this overview, however, let us reiterate something that is often lost amidst all the rhetorical hype. Firstly, the importance of the word and the printed page remains, but such importance is being *transformed* in relation to new technologies, new cultures, and new forms of life. Secondly, it will become increasingly more important to equip our students with a vision of the future of literacy, "a picture of the texts and discourses, skills and knowledges" that they might need, *and* their associated social and educational visions, rather than simple mastery of particular skills and methods (Luke & Elkins, 1998, p. 4; see also Luke, 1998). This has been described elsewhere as the "New Literacy Challenge" (Green, 1998), and requires consideration not just of the changing circumstances and conditions of literacy, learning and schooling but also of those enduring educational and social issues to do with fair and reasonable forms of access and equity, differential opportunity, and the practical production of the future (Kress, 1997).

Changing the scene of literacy

Recent emphases in literacy studies and literacy education include a recognition of sociocultural accounts and perspectives, as well as more explicit engagements with media culture and with the emergent technologies of information and communication.

Sociocultural issues are indicated in the way in which the rhetoric of "critical literacy," as it is called, has been taken up across the country, in policy at least. This development ostensibly brings together notions such as critical pedagogy and the socially critical school, as well as the so-called "critical thinking" movement. It similarly draws on programs such as the Disadvantaged Schools Program (DSP), as well as those addressed to issues such as gender equity and multiculturalism (and also, more recently, Aboriginal and Indigenous education). In NSW, as elsewhere (e.g., South

Australia), the work of Allan Luke and Peter Freebody and their various associates has been influential, as the basis for institutionalising a comprehensive sociocultural view of literacy in terms of code-breaking, text participation and usage, and textual analysis (Luke & Freebody, 1997, 1999). This has involved a particular rendering of the now well-known and well-established "text-content" model of language and literacy learning—something clearly evident in, for instance, the NSW K–6 Primary English Syllabus and its associated support documents.

The growing concern with media and technologies—part of a general media-shift in education and society (Green & Bigum, 1998)—is a more recent phenomenon, as we have already indicated. It is informed and even, to a significant degree, driven by increased awareness of *globalisation*, central to which is heightened concern for the cultural and economic effects of new technologies and new forms and dynamics of transnational communication and exchange. School education is not exempt from this. In NSW it has been mandated that, from 1999, all new teachers should have acquired specific computer "proficiencies" in the course and context of their initial teacher education and accreditation (NSW DET, 1997), and a large-scale program of inservice professional development in across-the-board educational computing has been initiated. The educational convergence of literacy and IT—or, more accurately, literacies and technologies—has been a marked feature of recent policy and pedagogic proposals alike (Lankshear et al., 1997). However, this is something still to be fully accepted or understood in school and classroom practice.

A significant problem with the new policy emphases on integrating IT into school education and literacy pedagogy has been a persistent *technocentrism*. This means an overly technicist or technical orientation in schools and curriculum, although often tempered by a constructivist view of learning. This is indicated by the way in which, all too often, programs of computer learning and professional development seem to endorse a "natural" movement from individualised skills-development, through a more or less technicist engagement with hardware and software, to due consideration for classroom applications and implications, after which comes a more reflective concern with "values and ethics" (NSW DET, 1997). Such a logic is at odds with contemporary literacy scholarship, which is sharply critical of "skills and methods" views of literacy pedagogy (Luke, 1998). This presents particular challenges for those advocating curriculum integration of literacy and IT, and hence for those seeking to implement such proposals. In this paper, accordingly, we suggest ways in which currently endorsed views of literacy learning and teaching can be articulated with recent developments in education and IT, and outline a model for curriculum integration and practice which effectively brings together sociocultural perspectives on literacy, IT and schooling.

Literacy in "3D"

Perhaps the strongest and most promising development of recent times has been the emergence of what can now be called a "situated social practice" model of language, literacy and technology learning—that is, an emphasis on situated, "authentic" learning and cultural apprenticeship, within a critical-sociocultural view of discourse and practice. This brings together established work in Australia addressed specifically to language and literacy learning (e.g., Boomer, 1988, 1989; Cambourne, 1988) with more recent work in literacy studies and the sociocultural paradigm, such as that of Gee (1990, 1991) and Lankshear (1997). Importantly, though, it explicitly stages a dialogue with "constructionist" work in computer culture and learning (Papert, 1980, 1993). This model was first developed in specific relation to subject-specific literacy learning (Green, 1988), and has been successfully deployed more recently in computer education (Green, 1996). The congruence between these otherwise disparate fields of practice suggests that the model in question here has a general relevance, as well as being specifically pertinent to the integration of literacy and IT in education. This was, in fact, the position adopted and endorsed in the "Digital Rhetorics" document (Lankshear et al., 1997; see also Lankshear, 1998 and Morgan, 1998).

In essence the model involves what can be called a "3D" view of literacy-technology learning. That is, it brings together three dimensions or aspects of learning and practice: the *operational*, the *cultural* and the *critical*. Rather than simply focusing on "how-to" knowledge, as it usually is understood—that is, technical competence and so-called "functional literacy"—it complements and supplements this by *contextualising* it, with due regard for matters of culture, history and power. This is a holistic, cultural-critical view of literacy-technology learning that takes explicitly into account contexts, contextuality and contextualisation (Lemke, 1995). The crucial point to emphasise here is that none of these dimensions of discourse and practice has any necessary priority over the others. All dimensions need to be addressed simultaneously, in an integrated view of literate practice and literacy pedagogy.

Importantly, this means that it is counter-productive, to say the least, to *start* with issues of "skill" or "technique," outside of an authentic context of situated social practice. That basic principle holds for all learning, whether it be learning school Geography, participating in an on-line professional development conference, or becoming competent with regard to some aspect of workplace practice. The model can be depicted thus:

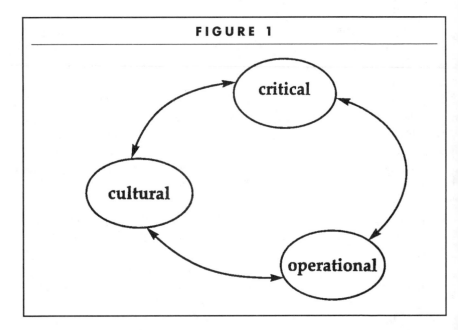

FIGURE 1

A comprehensive school program in literacy and IT needs to include, in both policy and practice, appropriate engagements with all three dimensions. This is something therefore to be explicitly incorporated into curriculum planning, at both the school level and that of the classroom.

Literacy: Integrating language, technology and learning

It is necessary to provide a more elaborated account of the model at this stage. To begin with, it derives from an integrated, sociocultural view of both language learning and technology learning. Following the work of Michael Halliday, language learning is seen as consisting of *learning lan-*

guage, learning through language and *learning about language.* This integrated view has been readily extended to technology learning (Boomer, 1987). A comprehensive school program addressed to the most effective and meaningful across-the-curriculum technology learning is one that emphasises equally *learning technology* (i.e. how to use technology), *learning through technology*, and *learning about technology*. It is for this reason we propose that literacy in this context is best understood as bringing together considerations of language, technology and learning. What needs to be emphasised is the importance of what Cambourne (1989, p. 20) describes as "acquisition learning" and Gee (1990) presents as the proper relationship between "acquisition" and "learning." The emphasis, then, must be on the priority of an experience- and activity-oriented curriculum over an instructional curriculum, or of teaching *for* learning over learning *from* teaching. Indeed, as Papert (1980, p. 6) observed some time ago, such a view has the potential to transform the way we understand and go about learning and teaching more generally. More importantly for our purposes here, it is consistent with the broadly constructivist view of curriculum and learning that has featured in progressive educational thinking in Australia since the 1970s.

The "3D" model assists us to conceptualise and plan such a curriculum. The *operational* dimension includes but also goes beyond received or usual notions of technical competence and "how-to" knowledge. Operational knowledge applies as much to literacy practice and learning as it does to IT practice and learning, and hence of course it applies with particular force to literacy-technology learning (or, rather, as it might be more appropriately expressed, *l(IT)eracy learning*). The issue here becomes how—literally—to operate the language system; how to make it work for one's own meaning-making purposes; how to "turn it on," etc. In the case of written language, the operational dimension involves understanding how the alphabet works and what it is, how graphemes and phonemes correspond, and to what extent, recognising the letters and subsequent formulations and conventions, and so on. It also involves learning the "mechanics" of handwriting and keyboarding, etc. For l(IT)eracy learning, the emphasis is on finding out how to make a computer operational, how to "turn it on" and make it "work," from the basics of making sure the cables are connected and switching it on to opening up files and documents, along with related activities such as opening and searching a database or using a CD-ROM.

Understanding and deploying the *cultural* dimension involves recognising and acknowledging that l(IT)erate practice and learning is always more than simply a matter of being able to operate language and technology systems, rather, such operational capacities are always in the specific service of authentic forms of meaning and practice. That is, we always use texts and technologies to do things in the world, and to achieve our own (and others') purposes, whether this be in the context of school or of work and everyday life. It follows that the emphasis is most appropriately placed on authentic contexts, forms and purposes of learning. To focus on the cultural dimension, therefore, is to focus on and give priority to matters of practice and meaning—the practice of meaning, or meaning-making, and the conduct and achievement of meaningful, effective practice.

The *critical* dimension draws in explicit consideration of context and history, and also of power. It takes into account that school knowledges are always partial and selective. They are always someone's "story," in the sense that the curriculum always represents some interests rather than others, and that it is a complex socio-historical construction. Rather than a single, universal Truth, the practice of curriculum and schooling follows lines of social division and is structured according to the prevailing principles of social organisation and power. Currently, a major concern for curriculum development and change is how to better or more appropriately represent the interests and experiences of Aboriginal and Indigenous populations and communities, in the spirit of reconciliation and social justice. This has definite implications for school literacy programs, whether it be in terms of beginning reading materials or social studies textbooks. For l(IT)eracy learning, teachers and students need similarly to be able to assess and evaluate software and other technology resources (e.g., databases, interactive CD-ROMs, the World Wide Web) in a spirit of informed scepticism. They need, that is, not only to be able to use such resources and to participate effectively and creatively in their associated cultures, but also to critique them, to read and use them against the grain, to appropriate and even re-design them.

Literacy models and frameworks: Re-mapping the territory

At this point it is important to make more explicit the terms of the articulation we are proposing here between literacy and IT in education and schooling, in accordance with the current state of policy and scholarship in NSW and elsewhere in Australia. As already mentioned, the NSW Literacy Strategy, along with contemporary English and literacy syllabus development in this State, clearly and firmly endorses a view of literacy curriculum that values explicitness, flexibility and comprehensiveness. As we have noted above, a central feature of that literacy curriculum is a socio-cultural approach to literacy learning. This is built around not only the notion that literacy is itself "an emergent technology—that is, a technology that changes the environment in which it is used" (Freebody, 1993, p. 48) but also that it is best understood in terms of an available repertoire of four "reading" roles or stances, each moreover with its own associated "technology." As Freebody (1993, p. 49) writes: "[A] successful reader needs to develop and sustain the resources to play four related roles: codebreaker, text-participant, text-user, and text-analyst." Further:

> [All] of these roles form part of successful reading as our culture currently demands it and...therefore any program of instruction in literacy, whether it be a kindergarten, in adult ESL classes, in university courses or at any points in between, needs to confront these roles systematically, explicitly, and at all developmental points. (Freebody, 1993, p. 58)

It is important to note that this account has itself been constantly revised. Importantly the notion of "roles" has tended to be subsumed in that of "resources," with this in turn to be understood more appropriately as referring in each instance to "a family of practices." What remains crucial however is the emphasis on covering and integrating a *repertoire* of capabilities, in sufficient breadth, depth and novelty (Luke & Freebody, 1999).

Two observations can be made here. Firstly, it is notable that the Luke and Freebody model implicitly associates "literacy" with "reading," and it has done so from the outset. The reference more particularly is to textual practice, to "texts," and to "what our culture expects, here and now, from people in their management of texts" (Freebody, 1993, p. 49). It can be argued that we need to emphasise *writing* more in literacy programs than is commonly the case. Certainly, recent scholarship suggests that writing—or, as it might be more properly expressed, production and design—needs to be foregrounded in the literacy curriculum (Kress, 1995, 1997; Lemke, 1989) especially in the context of the digital world and the networked society (Snyder, 1997). The second point to be made about the association here of literacy and reading is that such an account might be seen as mortgaged to *print* culture and literacy, that is, both print-bound and logocentric, in the sense that it is oriented to the language system and to written textuality. Although it certainly refers to the technologies of literacy, this is in more of a metaphorical sense than a literacy one (cf. Bruce, 1997; Green, 1993; McWilliam, 1996). Hence there is a resultant tendency to either take technology as such for granted or to imply an unwarranted neutrality for technology systems and technological practice. Among other things, this effectively closes off engagement with new and emergent literacies, which are increasingly organised and realised in mixed-mode, multimedia forms and contexts.

The value and advantage of the "3D" model proposed here is that, firstly, it was originally developed with specific regard to literacy, writing and school learning (Green, 1998), and secondly, it has been further developed with specific regard to computer learning, IT and education. In addition, it needs to be stressed that it is entirely consistent with the Freebody and Luke model and the critical-sociocultural paradigm. Just as that model has sought to put a socially critical perspective on the literacy agenda, the "3D" model does this for l(IT)eracy, and indeed the two have been developed concurrently and often in explicit dialogue with each other. It is useful, accordingly, to map the two on to each other:

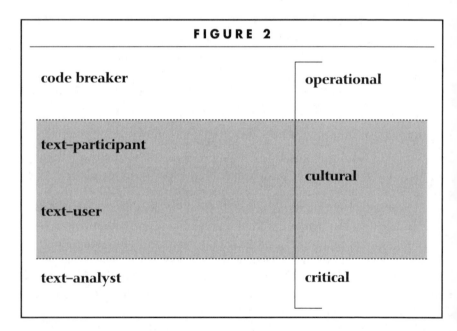

FIGURE 2

code breaker — operational

text–participant

text–user — cultural

text–analyst — critical

The important point to note is that, despite their congruence, the two models do not in actual fact exactly map onto each other: for instance, "operational" does not simply equate to "code-breaker." The relationship between the two is isomorphic and asymmetrical, with "roles" overlapping with "dimensions." In both cases, however, the principle of (ideal) simultaneity holds: Literate practice is, ideally, an integrated expression of *all* the roles and dimensions in question here, as two sides of the one conceptual coin. The implications for programming and planning, and indeed for assessment and evaluation, are considerable.

Literacy activities, across the various media, are always to be understood and practised across the full range of roles, resources, practices and dimensions. All too often, in sharp contrast, literacy programs are either unduly piecemeal and eclectic in this regard, or biased in actual practice and effect towards the operational and lower-order forms of "code-breaking," skills-development and text-participation, only occasionally or sporadically moving into the realm of text-usage. That was one of the key findings of the "Digital Rhetorics" project, in fact: most classrooms and most educational practice concentrated on operational activities, only sometimes taking effective account of the cultural dimension and rarely addressing the critical. This is notwithstanding policy and scholarly proposals to work with and across the full repertoire of literate-textual practice.

Classroom practice: Implications and applications

So how does this model translate into classroom practice? As with all such proposals and frameworks, there are no hard-and-fast rules or strict algorithms that make implementation and application either a simple or a straightforward matter. Teachers will always need to bring to bear their own professional expertise, their local knowledge, and their own programming skills, which is always therefore a matter of *re*-making personal-professional meaning of the model outlined here, so that it works for them. Moreover, as noted in the "Digital Rhetorics" report:

> [How] we come to understand technology-mediated practices, and how we integrate new technologies into literacy-mediated practices, will depend on what we encounter in the way of practice—*wherever* and *whenever* we encounter it. Whatever our intentions as teachers may be about "covering" each of the operational, cultural and critical dimensions of literacy within our programs and relating them to each other as integral aspects of literacy, it is how literacy practices are *experienced* by learners that really matters. Similarly, the fact that a social practice involving new technologies is experienced by learners under very difficult and challenging conditions does not obviate the fact that *what* is experienced (under these conditions) will have a very important impact on what that social practise is seen to comprise—and hence, what "it" is learned as. (Lankshear et al., 1997, p. 110 [Vol. 2])

This is an important cautionary note to keep in mind. Learning and teaching are always situated *and* situating, productive, generating their own local, distinctive effects. Nonetheless it is possible to make some suggestions here about how to go about integrating the "3D" model into classroom and school life.

The first of these is *the priority, in practice, of the cultural dimension.* This means putting the emphasis firmly and clearly on authentic meaning-making and meaningful, appropriate action within a given community of practice. In the case of classrooms and schools, this puts the focus on meaningful and appropriate school and classroom learning—on "doing school," as best one can, something that applies equally to students and to teachers. Ideally, and preferably, "doing school" is always linked to and in the service of "real-life" and "life-like" social practices. Moreover, in the context of what is admittedly an expanded view of literacy pedagogy:

> In a sociocultural approach, the focus of learning and education is not children, nor schools, but human lives viewed as trajectories through multiple social practices in various social institutions. If learning is to be effacacious, then what a child or an adult does now as a learner must be connected in meaningful and motivating ways with "mature" (insider) versions of related social practices. (Gee, Hull, & Lankshear, 1996, p. 4)

The challenge here lies in making schools and classrooms, as much as possible, into "worldly," socially meaningful and relevant places, characterised by what Jo-Anne Reid (1997, p. 150) has described as *generic practice*: "the engaged production of social texts for real purposes." That has always been the strength, in fact, of recent "progressive" proposals for Australian literacy education, featured in the work of educators such as Brian Cambourne and Garth Boomer as much as that of Peter Freebody, Pam Gilbert and Barbara Comber.

Putting the emphasis on the cultural dimension of school l(IT)eracy practices means taking full account of the specificity of the *educational* activity in question, whether it be subject-area learning (e.g., Mathematics or Social Studies) or learning how to read (and have fun!) through an engagement with e-books and CD-ROMs (e.g., the "Living Books" series). This remains the case, of course, even when there are no "new technologies" involved—which only accentuates the point that what we are concerned with here, above all else, is authentic educational practice. Whatever the lesson or unit of work, or the level of schooling, the teaching task and the challenge is finding ways of enabling and encouraging learners to enter into particular communities of practice, discourse and inquiry; how to become an "insider" in the culture of the Science classroom, for instance, and how to be an effective member of and active participant in that culture, able to engage productively in its textual and other practices. In Gee's terms, this involves entering into the secondary Discourse of the subject-area or the educational activity in question. In involves becoming identified *and* identifying oneself as "a member of a socially meaningful group, or 'social network'...to signal (that one is playing) a socially meaningful 'role' within that Discourse community" (Gee, 1990, p. 143).[5]

The value of such a view of learning and teaching is firstly that it puts education firmly up front, and that means emphasising literacy and curriculum issues in the classroom and in one's teaching, rather than technology or technical issues. In such a view, the latter are always secondary, or *supplementary*, although importantly never neutral. Technologies *support* learning and teaching, which always remains the main game, and indeed the point of the whole exercise. Hence it is teachers' *educational* expertise that needs to be foregrounded and strengthened, along with their professional knowledge, skills and dispositions, which they then bring to bear on the challenge of the new technologies for schooling and for education more generally. Among other things, this restores the role and the significance of good teaching, and of the teacher as "expert" in his or her own classroom, charged with drawing children into the culture of learning.

Hence, integrating IT into the Key Learning Areas (KLAs) always, and of necessity, involves drawing on the specific subject-area expertise of teachers. Similarly, constructing coherent, informed, effective literacy programs requires that teachers' professional judgement and their own theories of literacy *and* pedagogy become crucial, first-order resources for curriculum and professional development. Policy-wise, it follows that strategic alliances need to be forged, within schools, between different but related communities of interest and expertise, and new opportunities generated for across-the-curriculum professional dialogue.

Secondly, such a view both contextualises and prepares the ground for more effective realisations of both the operational and the critical dimensions of literacy. In the case of the operational dimension, what emerges from such

---

[5] As Gee writes (1990, p. 143): "A Discourse is a socially accepted association among ways of using adult language, of thinking, feeling, believing, valuing, and of acting"—for instance, for our purposes here, as a primary-school student, an adult ESL student, or a student of HSC Geography. See also Lankshear (1998, pp. 51–53).

an approach is that skills development can now more readily be seen as meaningful and relevant, because it becomes clear that having appropriate, socially recognisable "skills" and the like is imperative in order to function effectively within that particular Discourse context. In today's world, perhaps more so than ever before, this especially means communication of "symbolic-analytic" skills—not just those such as spelling or keyboarding but also those associated with design, critical analysis and electronic and other forms of information access and handling.

With regard to the critical dimension, it is important to bear in mind that social and educational practices need to be "meaningful" before they can become "critical," or be made so. This is often forgotten, or overlooked. Becoming an informed, effective "insider" of a given community of practice is crucial, and that is achieved most powerfully through immersion, usage and engagement—through generic, cultural practice and "naturalistic," authentic learning. But it is arguably not enough simply to be an "insider" in this fashion, however effective one might be in that regard. James Gee and others note that this needs to be supplemented and extended by a *critical* perspective, one which asks reflexive questions about that culture and that community, and about who one is expected to be and become accordingly. As Freebody (1993, p. 57) writes:

> [E]ven if you, as reader, can successfully decode [a] text, can successfully comprehend it, relating it to your social knowledge, and can successfully take part in literacy activities that my be based on such a text, a fully successful reading...calls for nothing less than an analysis of the ways in which the text constructs a version of you, the reader.

And, by extension, of the community you are participating in and thereby helping to construct and to sustain. Moreover, this is something that holds, whatever the level of schooling or the nature of the literate activity in question. But it is also the case that one needs to be able to use texts effectively and participate in their associated cultures—from the "inside," as it were—*if* critique and analysis is to be meaningful and relevant, *and* grounded in practice.

Conclusion

As a final note, we want to point briefly to the example of the home page, both as representative of a new l(IT)eracy practice and as a possible curriculum focus for teachers' programming and students' learning (cf. Morgan, 1998, pp. 149–151). There seems little doubt, as education becomes increasingly technologised and globally referenced, that the always editable practice of the home page will feature more and more in classroom and school practice, as a gateway to the world and as a marker of on-going, identity-work. Not only does it constitute a new "text type"— individual and collective, local and global—and a distinctive new literacy challenge, bringing together rhetoric and design, but it also opens up new possibilities for learning and exchange—and also, of course, new dangers, such as those associated with the market and the image. Teachers need to see themselves as artful intermediaries in this regard, negotiating the transition between residual, dominant and emergent textual cultures, ushering our young people in a principled, mindful way into new wor(l)d orders, and equipping them to understand *and* critique them. This requires a holistic, integrated view of literacy and learning in new times, one which brings operational, cultural and critical knowledges, in the service of active meaning-making and a just and sustainable future for all of us.

Meeting the challenge of new forms of textual practice and media culture and new relations between literacy and IT is likely to play an ever-increasingly significant role in teachers' professional lives, as indeed in society more generally. Already today's young people are moving confidently into the future in this regard, more often than not influenced and resourced by media practices and networks and by the entertainment industry—to date much more so, it can be argued, than by their schooling. There is definitely a task here for teachers and for schools, and an obligation. However, we are just beginning to find appropriate, informed ways of being both pro-active and critically pragmatic in rising to and meeting this challenge, and it is likely that this will continue to exercise the profession and the education industry for some time to come. Frameworks, overviews and proposals such as outlined in this article hopefully can contribute to the work of rethinking and "re-tooling" that is required of educators generally and also of the wider community.

REFERENCES

Australian Bureau of Statistics. (1999). Use of the Internet by householders, Australia. In *ABS Catalogue* No. 8147.0 August. Commonwealth of Australia, Canberra. http://www.statistics.gov.au

Australian Labor Party. (1995). *Labor's plans for school education.* Australian Labor Party Election Policy Document, Australian Labor Party, Sydney.

Bigum, C. (1993). Curriculum and the new mythinformation technologies. In B. Green (Ed.), *Curriculum, technology and textual practice* (pp. 81–105). Geelong: Deakin University.

Boomer, G. (1987). Technology, curriculum and learning. In G. Boomer, *Changing education* (pp. 20–29). Canberra: Commonwealth Schools Commission.

Boomer, G. (1988). *Metaphors and meanings: Essays on English teaching by Garth Boomer*, Ed. B. Green. Adelaide Australian Association for the Teaching of English.

Boomer, G. (1989). Literacy: The epic challenge beyond progressivism. *English in Australia, 89*, 6–17.

Bruce, B. (1997). Literacy technologies: What stance should we take? *Journal of Literacy Research, 29*(2), 289–309.

Bruce, B. (1998). New literacies. *Journal of Adolescent & Adult Literacy, 42*(1), pp. 46–49.

Cambourne, B. (1988). *The whole story: Natural learning and the acquisition of literacy in the classroom*. Auckland: Ashton Scholastic.

Cambourne, B. (1989). Look what they done to my song, Ma: A reply to Luke, Baty and Stephens. *English in Australia, 90*, 13–22.

Christie, F. (1990). The changing face of literacy. In F. Christie (Ed.), *Literacy for a changing world* (pp. 26–53). Hawthorn, Victoria, Australian Council for Educational Research.

Christie, F. (Ed.). (1990). *Literacy for a changing world*. Hawthorn, Victoria, Australian Council for Educational Research.

Christie, F., Devlin, B., Freebody, P., Luke, A., Martin, J., Threadgold, T., & Walton, C. (1991). *Teaching English literacy: A project of National Significance on the Preservice Preparation of Teachers for Teaching English Literacy*. Centre for Studies in Language and the Department of Employment, Education and Training [The Christie Report]. Darwin: Northern Territory University.

Christie, F., & Misson, R. (Eds.). (1998). *Literacy and schooling*. London and New York, Routledge.

CommerceNet. (1999). *Internal statistics: The CommerceNet/Nielson Internet demographic survey*, http://www.commerce.net.

Department of Employment Education and Training (DEET). (1991). *Australia's language: The Australian language and literacy policy, companion volume to the policy paper*. Canberra: Australian Government Publishing Service.

Dirkson, D. (1998, April). Direction of the WWW. In *Techsetter Magazine: The Millennium*. http://www.techsetter.com

Freebody, P. (1993). A socio-cultural approach: Resourcing four roles as a literacy learner. In A Badenhop & A. Watson (Eds.), *Prevention of reading failure* (pp. 48–60). Sydney: Ashton-Scholastic.

Gee, J.P. (1990). *Sociolinguistics and literacies: Ideologies in discourse*. London: Falmer Press.

Gee, J. (1991). What is literacy? In C. Mitchell & K. Weiler (Eds.), *Rewriting literacy* (pp. 1–11). New York: Bergin & Garvey.

Gee, J., Hull, G., & Lankshear, C. (1996). *The new work order: Behind the language of the new capitalism*. Sydney: Allen & Unwin.

Green, B. (1988). Subject-specific literacy and school learning: A focus on writing. *Australian Journal of Education, 32*(2), 156–179.

Green, B. (1993). Curriculum, technology, textual practice: Images and issues. In B. Green (Ed.), *Curriculum, technology and textual practice* (pp. 9–31). Geelong: Deakin University.

Green, B. (1996, July). *Literacy/technology/learning: Notes and issues*. Discussion paper prepared for the DEETYA Digital Rhetorics Project, Brisbane.

Green, B. (1998). *The new literacy challenge?* Keynote address delivered to the Literacy and Technology Conference, Armidale Regional Office of the NSW Department of Education and Training, Armidale.

Green, B., & Bigum, C. (1996). Hypermedia or media hype? New technologies and the future of literacy education. In G. Bull & M. Anstey (Eds.), *The literacy lexicon* (pp. 193–204). Sydney: Prentice-Hall.

Green, B., & Bigum, C. (1998). Re-tooling schooling? Information technology, cultural change and the future(s) of Australian education. In J. Smyth, R. Hattam, & M. Lawson (Eds.), *Schooling for a fair go* (pp. 71–96). Annandale: The Federation Press.

Hoffman, D., & Novak, T. (1999). The evolution of the digital divide: Examining the relationship of race to internet access and usage over time, Project 2000. Owen Graduate School of Management, Vanderbilt University, May, http://www2000. ogsm.vanderbilt.edu.

Hoskin, K. (1993). Technologies of learning and alphabetic culture: The history of writing as the history of education. In B. Green (Ed.), *The insistence of the letter: Literacy studies and curriculum theorizing* (pp. 27–45). London and Washington, DC: The Falmer Press.

Kress, G. (1995). *Writing the future: English and the making of a culture of innovation.* Sheffield, National Association of Teachers of English.

Kress, G. (1997). *Before writing: Rethinking the paths to literacy.* London and New York: Routledge.

Lankshear, C. (1997). *Changing literacies.* Buckingham and Philadelphia: Open University Press.

Lankshear, C. (1998). Frameworks and workframes: Literacy policies and new orders. *Unicorn,* 24(2), 43–58.

Lankshear, C., Bigum, C., Durrant, C., Green, B., Honan, E., Morgan, W., Murray, J., Snyder, I., & Wild, M. (1997). *Digital rhetorics: Literacies and technologies in education—current practices and future directions* (Volumes 1–3 plus Executive Summary). Canberra: Department of Employment, Education, Training and Youth Affairs.

Lemke, J. (1989). Social semiotics: A new model for literacy education. In D. Bloome (Ed.), *Classrooms and literacy.* Norwood, NJ: Ablex Publishing.

Lemke, J. (1995). *Textual politics: Discourse and social dynamics.* London: Taylor and Francis.

Lo Bianco, J., & Freebody, P. (1997). *Australian literacies: Informing national policy on literacy education.* Canberra: Language Australia.

Luke, A. (1998). Getting over method: Literacy teaching as work in "New Times." *Language Arts,* 75(4), 305–313.

Luke, A., & Elkins, J. (1998). Reinventing literacy in "new times." *Journal of Adolescent & Adult Literacy,* 42(1), 4–7.

Luke, A., & Freebody, P. (1997). Shaping the social practices of reading. In S. Muspratt, A. Luke, & P. Freebody (Eds.), *Constructing critical literacies: Teaching and learning textual practice* (pp. 185–226). Creskill, NJ: Hampton Press.

Luke, A., & Freebody, P. (1999). Further notes on the four resources model, *Reading Online,* http://www.readingonline.org/research/lukefreebody.html.

McWilliam, E. (1996). Pedagogies, technologies, bodies. In E. McWilliam & P. Taylor (Eds.), *Pedagogy, technology and the body* (pp. 1–22). New York: Peter Lang.

Morgan, W. (1998). Old letteracy or new literacy: Reading and writing the wor(l)d on-line. In F. Christie & R. Misson (Eds.), *Literacy and schooling* (pp. 129–154). London and New York: Routledge.

NSW Department of Education and Training. (1997). *Computer proficiency for teachers.* Sydney: Department of Education and Training Coordination.

NSW Department of School Education. (1997). *Focus on literacy.* Sydney, NSW: Department of School Education, Curriculum Directorate.

Papert, S. (1980). *Mindstorms: Children, computers and powerful ideas.* New York: Basic Books.

Papert, S. (1993). *The children's machine: Rethinking school in the age of the computer.* New York: Basic Books.

Parliament of Commonwealth of Australia. (1991). *Australia as an information society: Grasping new paradigms.* Report of the House of Representatives Standing Committee for Long Term Strategies. Canberra: Australian Government Publishing Service.

Reid, J. (1997). Generic practice. *Australian Journal of Language and Literacy, 20*(2), 148–155.

Rizvi, F., & Lingard, B. (1997). Foreword. In I. Snyder (Ed.), *Page to screen: Taking literacy into the electronic era.* Sydney: Allen & Unwin.

Snyder, I. (Ed.). (1997). *Page to screen: Taking literacy into the electronic era.* Sydney: Allen & Unwin.

Techsetter. (1998). Schools and teachers get connected. In *Techsetter Magazine: New Year's Resolutions,* January. http://www.techsetter.com.

Critical Literacy Book Reviews

**Stephens, J. (1992). *Language and ideology in children's fiction.*
London: Longman.**
Reviewed by Mary Rhodes. (1993). *The Australian Journal of Language and
Literacy*, 16(4), 363–364.

John Stephens' thought provoking exploration of the ideology implicit in children's fiction is firmly founded on principles of critical literacy
and will appeal to anyone who is concerned about the dangers of reader
response approaches which stress the need to identify with characters.
For Stephens this method implies textual subjegation of the reader and
overstates the importance of verisimilitude, thus masking the processes of
the textual production of meaning.

The book deals with complex concepts in a most clear and concise
way. The introduction links his work to methods of discourse analysis
used by Fairclough in *Language and Power* (1989), but points out that
Stephens is looking more specifically at the discourse of narrative fiction
for children and between infancy and early adolescence. To do this he
has formulated a new interdisciplinary methodology combining insights
from contemporary critical linguistics and narrative and literary theory.

The first four chapters give a detailed argument for more critical approaches to studying literature by considering ideology, subjectivity, intertextuality and the way "carnivalesque" texts, by denying simple empathy,
situate readers outside the narrative. Chapter One considers ideology in
fiction and the way it can be both deliberate and implicit. Children's fiction
is intended to socialize its target audience, since through narrative, society
inculcates values. The most powerful vehicles for the ideology contained
in all narrative are the texts where ideological positions are implicit and
therefore seem natural. Through a detailed analysis of the discourse of a
"simple" four line poem by Roger McGough, *Hide and Seek*, Stephens shows
how a text can create a subject position for its readers. He continues with
a close analysis of the power of narrative structure.

The relationship between a reader and text is seen as similar to the
relationship between the subject (or individual) and society, in that the

reader may be constituted by a range of available subject positions or choose which position to adopt. Thus, while a text strives to construct subject positions through the process of focalization, a reader may oppose these positions.

Chapters Three and Four advocate a playful engagement with the text, involving practices such as the study of intertextuality and "carnivalesque" texts which oppose authoritarianism and often parody mainstream literary genres. Such texts encourage shifting subject positions and discourage simple identification with the main character. The narrator is often playfully intrusive and the unthinking acceptance of ideology is problematized.

The final three chapters look at three different forms of children's literature: picture books, historical fiction and fantasy. Stephens concludes with an illuminating discussion of fantasy and realism, but in spite of the many differences, he points out that both modes construct ideologically infused subject positions for their readers.

A brief review cannot do justice to the scholarship of Stephens' book. Far from being a dry exposition of contemporary literary theory, his arguments are illustrated by many examples from a vast array of literature for young people. Each chapter has a summarizing conclusion and enough suggestions for future work to inspire research for years to come. I strongly recommend it to anyone interested in teaching students to read critically.

Janks, H. (1993). *Language & position and language, identity and power.* Johannesburg, South Africa: University Press and Hodder & Stoughton Educational.
Reviewed by John Davidson. (1999). *Practically Primary,* 4(3), 45–46.

Hilary Janks and her work featured at the ALEA/AATE National Conferences in Adelaide, July 1999. Not just a keynote speaker—a genuine *highlight.*

At a pre-conference workshop she and Pat Thomson led 25 teachers through a whole day of deconstruction, unpacking and analysing texts, talking and listening, taking up positions, telling stories, uncovering meanings, and finally *reconstructing* texts to reposition ourselves.

Phew! It sounds heavy, but I couldn't wait to get back to the classroom to try some of this stuff out. Now I've got these workbooks written by Hilary a few years ago, part of a series she's edited called the Critical Language Awareness Series. As she says in the introduction:

All the workbooks deal with the relationship between language and power. This relationship is not obvious and so the materials attempt to raise awareness of the way in which language can be used and is used to maintain and to challenge existing forms of power. There can be little doubt that power matters....

She gives an overview of what she means by critical language awareness, and a page of "suggested methods for teachers." She looks at identity, position, point of view, the way we use language to position other people, context, learning to read critically, and so on.

None of this is dense or "academic," although it does require interpretation because it is explicitly set in the South African context. The materials and activities are also more suited to secondary classes and need to be "translated" for use by primary teachers. That's to say, they can't be used "off the shelf" or "just before lunch on Wednesday" and so we classroom teachers need to think seriously about what we're doing with our kids.

Burns, A., & Hood, S. (1998). *Teaching critical literacy* (Teachers' Voices 3). New South Wales, Australia: National Centre for English Language Teaching and Research, Macquarie University.
Reviewed by Ronda Schloithe. (1999). *The Australian Journal of Language and Literacy*, 22(3), 253–254.

One of the key theoretical ideas to emerge from recent debates about literacy, language learning and ESL development has been the notion of critical literacy. This text, the third volume in the Teachers' Voices series, provides a useful resource for teachers wanting to explore pedagogical models for teaching critical literacy, and reflect upon the theoretical and practical questions emanating from applying this approach to ESL teaching.

The text centres upon action research undertaken by a collaborative group of six South Australian Adult Migrant English program (AMEP) teachers investigating, within their own contexts, approaches to teaching critical literacy to second language learners at different stages of learning. Carried out in 1996 through the National Centre for English Language Teaching and Research, their action research encompasses several questions.

- What is meant by critical literacy?
- What kinds of cultural assumptions are embedded in the notion of critical literacy?
- Can critical literacy only be taught to advanced students?

- If not, how can critical literacy be developed with students at various levels?
- What kinds of teaching materials need to be identified or developed to teach critical literacy?

(p. iv)

Section One, subtitled "Researching Critical Literacy," contains a paper by each of the research co-ordinators and the editors of this text. The first of these, by Anne Burns, highlights the ever-demanding role of teachers as curriculum developers, stressing both the interrelationships between theory, research and classroom practice, and the professional development benefits of undertaking action research. Based upon questions consistently raised by AMEP teachers with whom Burns has worked, this paper offers: an explicit sense of how to develop an action research focus; critical questions to ask; and methods for collecting and analysing/interpreting data as well as for ensuring that validity and reliability are addressed. It also suggests ways for sharing with wider audiences any insights gained.

The second paper, by Susan Hood, identifies the theoretical frameworks which have given rise to the notion of critical pedagogy and the different interpretations applied to this. Using recent research findings, Hood examines what a critical approach to reading is in relation to other dominant approaches and describes some accounts of practices being advocated as starting points for critical analysis of texts. The question of student resistance to critical reading—especially when students are from cultural traditions where resisting either texts or teachers is not considered appropriate—is raised, and the importance of students seeing the potential for their own multiple readings of texts reinforced.

Section Two, detailing the teachers' accounts, attempts to answer questions such as the following:

- How can critical literacy approaches be taught at the beginning ESL levels?
- To what extent are any interpretations of texts by individual students legitimate responses?
- How does the teacher deal with the mismatch between the cultural knowledge assumed in the text and that which the student brings to the reading?

Each account outlines the teaching context, research focus questions, and the class goals/aims, along with detailed descriptions and actual examples of activities undertaken with students. A summary of personal/processional reflections on processes and insights and lists of discussion/classroom tasks arising from the research are included.

This "user friendly" text provides an avenue for clarifying definitions of critical thinking and the assumptions made in integrating this into teaching/learning contexts.

Although designed with adult second language learners in mind, the activities used by each teacher would be appropriate for middle primary school to tertiary teaching settings. These activities utilise oral and written texts, many of which involve student-centres and local community issues. Written media, junk mail, and information texts are used to advantage, although electronic texts do not appear to be a priority. And because each activity is described within the context of the teacher's purposes for using these, there is a clear sense of how and why these activities assist in the development of particular aspect of critical literacy.

Above all, this text celebrates practitioners' efforts to understand "theoretical debates but explore them in the practical and complex context of the classroom" (p. 17), thereby continuing the practice, established in previous volumes of the Teachers' Voices series, of affirming the value and necessity of classroom-based action research. Of clear relevance to teachers who work with adult second language learners, it confronts many fundamental questions faced by those attempting to teach critical literacy to all learners, and is therefore recommended as a relevant resource for the wider audience.

Knobel, M., & Healy, A. (Eds.). (1998). *Critical literacies in the primary classroom*. Rozelle, New South Wales, Australia: Primary English Teaching Association.
Reviewed by Jane Leaker. (1999). *Practically Primary*, 4(3), 44–45.

Critical literacies in the primary classroom consists of an introductory chapter describing what critical literacy is and then the practical experiences of eight experienced educators working with children of all primary age groups.

The introduction is a very pleasant surprise. After reading it I felt that I had a good understanding of what critical literacy was. The authors have done an excellent job in demystifying terminology that in the past has put me off reading further into similar texts. Even though the authors say you can skip this chapter as it is largely theory, it is very important that readers do read it. I believe that to understand the practice they need to understand the theory behind it.

The goal stated in the introduction reads as follows: "to present different ways of doing critical literacy in connection with everyday literacy practices." I believe that this goal was well and truly met. In each chapter where each experience was described the connection between critical literacy and context was very evident. The most striking and inspirational example of this were the experiences of a classroom teacher working with the Woody Kids as described by Annah Healy in Chapter 3. Here it is most evident that the social, economic and cultural background of the children in your class should determine the everyday literacy events your students engage in.

Highlighted throughout is the need for teachers to work in context. The experiences described in this book can't just be transferred to your classroom but they can make you think about what you could do in your own situation. If you are only thinking about, or beginning to use, critical literacy in your classroom then Chapter 8 would be a good starting point. In this chapter Michele Knobel describes the work she does with teacher education students. As well as providing the theoretical knowledge base there are numerous possible approaches to critical literacy in the classroom.

This is a valuable resource for the classroom teacher. It gives you the who, what, how, why, and when of critical literacy. As teachers are very busy people and don't have the time to wade through complex texts they will find this text easy to read, practical and in some instances inspirational.

Lohrey, A. (1998) *Critical literacy: A professional development resource*. Melbourne, Australia: Language Australia.
Reviewed by John Davidson. (1999). *Practically Primary*, 4(3), 45.

This little book is a gem! It's not really "for the classroom," it's more a staff development resource. But if your PD coordinator baulks at spending $12.50 for a 28 page booklet, ring Language Australia and get one yourself.

Dr. Lohrey provides background support material for workshops "doing" critical literacy, for example, he describes seven "contexts of text"— situation, form, author(s), voice, genre, rhetorical strategies and world view.

He notes two kinds of meaning (and therefore knowledge) constructed in texts—*implicit* and *explicit*—arranged as a pyramid (or a sort of iceberg) of meaning. The bit you normally see "on top" is just the explicit tip. "The largest proportion of the meaning we construct will be hidden, implicit and contextual" (p. 26).

The purpose of critical literacy...is to make the permanent foundations of the pyramid...more flexible and accessible to conscious and explicit use.

There's also a terrific—and readily available—reference list. Highly recommended!

Dally, S. (1998). *Civics and citizenship: we will take part: Teaching civics and citizenship* and the companion glossary *The ABC of being a critically literate citizen*. Adelaide, South Australia: Department of Education, Training and Employment.
Reviewed by Kerry Kavanagh. (1999). *Practically Primary*, 4(3), 46–47.

Those of you who have had the privilege of using some of Shirley Dally's earlier curriculum materials (*Gender perspectives*, 1995 and *Girls and boys come out to play*, 1996) will share my excitement about the prospect of more material becoming available. You won't be disappointed with her latest materials *Civics and citizenship: we will take part: Teaching civics and citizenship* and its companion glossary: *The ABC of being a critically literate citizen*. These materials use the English Statement and Studies of Society and Environment as the basis for teaching about civics and citizenship. They are primary designed for use with students in Year 4–7 but as the foreword points out, they "can easily be adapted for the early years or for secondary schooling." These are the type of literacy curriculum materials that rise to the challenge set by Luke and Freebody in their recent article in *Practically Primary* namely that literacy teaching should be:

about the kind of literate practices that are needed to enhance peoples' agency over their life trajectories and to enhance communities' intellectual, cultural and semiotic resources in print/multi-mediated economies.
(Luke & Freebody, Vol 4, No 2, 1999)

While teachers can readily agree with the challenge set by Luke and Freebody, putting it into practice is not such an easy task. This is where Dally's materials come into their own. She takes on the hard topics and demonstrates ways that these topics can be explored constructively with students. The power of these curriculum materials is that they don't assume that the reader has access to the same information as the developer. While not being condescending it does provide explicit support and opportunities:

...for students to practise how to exercise agency and make decisions about what can be useful and pleasurable without being harmful, and also about what may need to be resisted or changed.

(Dally, 1999:9)

Barton, D., Hamilton, M., & Ivanic, R. (Eds.). (1999). *Situated literacies: Reading and writing in context.* London: Routledge.
Reviewed by Rosie Kerin. (2000). *The Australian Journal of Language and Literacy, 23*(2), 169–171.

What do media images of literacy practices as diverse as bilingual Welsh farmers at livestock auctions, Catholic parish newsletters preparing first communicants, and the material processes and products of primary students undertaking project work at home have in common? Very little you might say, but they are in fact all subjects of research reported on in *Situated Literacies: Reading and Writing in Context.* These and other equally diverse topics in this book have as their focus literacies that "are positioned in relation to the social institutions and power relations that sustain them" (p. 1).

The editors of this book, the Literacy Research Group at Lancaster University, have collaborated with three other literacy researchers, Jim Gee, Denny Taylor and Janet Maybin, to produce this book which has as its starting point the "New Literacies Studies." This movement, or framework as they describe it, explores literacy as a social practice whereby there is "a 'social turn' away from a focus on individuals and 'private' minds to a focus on knowledge, words and deeds in their local, social, cultural and political contexts" (p. 5).

The background and development of the New Literacies Studies are detailed as an introduction, placing the research projects in their particular contexts, and this provides a useful backdrop for what is to follow. Propositions about the nature of literacy practice viewed from a social perspective are identified: "It presents a view of literacy as multiple, patterned by power relations, purposeful, historically situated, and changing over time" (p. 2). Each of the research projects deals with one or more of these propositions, and given the scope and different emphases within the book, a summary of these projects may be useful:

- Media images of literacy; exploring literacy as social practice. *Mary Hamilton*

- New literacies and time: Catholic parish newsletters. *Karin Tusting*

- Third space theory; borderland discourse and the "in-between" literacies and prison. *Anita Wilson*
- Farmers' literacy and discourse practices while engaging in agricultural bureaucracy at livestock auctions. *Kathryn Jones*
- Physical characteristics of children's project work. *Fiona Ormerod and Ro Ivanic*
- Family literacy projects in Britain. *Kathy Pitt*
- ESL university students using computer-mediated conferencing. *Renata de Pourbaix*
- "Symmetry" in researching literacy and student writing: Writing practices of environmental science students and tutors' responses. *Simon Pardoe*
- Researching literacy practices: Students researching their own literacies in their social contexts. *David Barton*

Reflexivity and the links between research, teaching and learning are emphasised throughout, as are the political dimensions of literacy. Jim Gee stresses the importance of highlighting these political dimensions:

> Many of us involved in the "social turn" assumed that the movements that made it up were somehow inherently politically "progressive." That is, we assumed that focusing on the social would unmask the workings of hierarchy, power and social injustice, as well as create more humane, less elitist and individualistic, institutions (e.g., schools) and communities. (p. 185)

He argues that, instead, the new global and technological capitalism has harnessed the social turn to describe human worth in terms of productivity and "value-added" dimensions of workers. Workers are rewarded for total commitment, performance excellence and blurring the line between their private and business lives. He suggests that the New Literacies Studies could be more powerful politically if it researched the sites at which new capitalism operates. He argues that the structure for workers in the new capitalism is "lean and mean," resulting in employment that is poorly paid and temporary, and that the elite—or as he calls them the "enchanted workers"—have more in common with their international counterparts than they do with the temporal and services workers they manage. Barton urges researchers to focus more closely on the political and economic ramifications of the embedded literacies in the context of workers and their literacy and discursive practices.

Following Gee's exploration of the political dimensions, Tusting, Ivanic and Wilson establish links between the research projects outlined and make suggestions for further research. The chapter "New Literacy Studies at the Interchange" calls for readers to consider following directions they outline "either by taking the routes we have signposted here or by finding new routes and directions of their own" (p. 218).

I believe that this book will be of particular interest to those interested in such research, but it also has much to offer teachers who are not intending to carry out formal research. In particular, the research on school projects, the creation of "virtual space" through student emails, and David Barton's chapter dealing with students researching their own situated literacies as pedagogical tools make fascinating reading and relate directly to classroom contexts.

Although some of the issues explored in the book are quite complex and without final resolution, the book is highly readable and engaging.

You may also like to visit the website of the Literacy Research Group at Lancaster University: http://www.literacy.lancs.ac.uk/.